DATE DUE

NOV 2 0 1998	
NOV 2 2 2000	
DEC - 2001	
NOV 1 4 2001	
NOV 2 1 2003	

Assisted Suicide

A Decision-Making Guide for Health Professionals

Stephen Jamison

Jossey-Bass Publishers • San Francisco

Substantial discounts on bulk quantities of Jossey-Bass books are available to corporations, professional associations, and other organizations. For details and discount information, contact the special sales department at Jossey-Bass Inc., Publishers (415) 433–1740; Fax (800) 605–2665.

For sales outside the United States, please contact your local Simon & Schuster International Office.

Jossey-Bass Web address: http://www.josseybass.com

 Manufactured in the United States of America on Lyons Falls Turin Book. This paper is acid-free and 100 percent totally chlorine-free.

Library of Congress Cataloging-in-Publication Data

Jamison, Stephen.
    Assisted suicide : a decision-making guide for health
professionals / Stephen Jamison. — 1st ed.
      p.   cm.
    Includes bibliographical references and index.
    ISBN 0-7879-0873-8 (alk. paper)
    1. Assisted suicide.   2. Terminal care—Decision making.
I. Title.
    [DNLM: 1. Suicide, Assisted.   2. Ethics, Medical.   3. Decision
Making.   W 50 J32a   1997]
    R726.J357   1997
    179.7—dc21
    DNLM/DLC
    for Library of Congress   97-29352

FIRST EDITION
HB Printing   10 9 8 7 6 5 4 3 2 1

Contents

To Joshua and Sarah

Acknowledgments

No book is ever written in a vacuum. Books, like their authors, are products of countless personal and professional influences. This book certainly could not have been written without those who have journeyed with me during various stages of the work.

I owe a great debt to Steve Heilig, with whom I long ago began debating the pros and cons of assisted suicide. I thank him for his continuing friendship and support.

I would like to express particular thanks to the many clinicians who, over the years, were willing to patiently share their ideas and concerns with me. I appreciate especially the long-standing support of Bill Anderek, Bill Atchley, Kate Christensen, and Guy Micco. Many of the thoughts in this book have their source in random comments these compassionate physicians once made at conferences or ethics committee meetings. I only hope that when my own final time comes, such a clinician will be standing by my bedside, working on my behalf for a peaceful, humane death.

Most of the other physicians, nurses, mental health professionals, and hospice personnel who have contributed to my understanding of this subject will have to remain nameless here, but I must single out Gary Johanson and Brad Stuart, two remarkably thoughtful hospice clinicians, who opened their souls to me on this issue.

Among others who were there when I needed them and have earned my gratitude is Gary Hamilton—a clinician of the intellect—who taught me more than the basics about writing and thinking.

But books are not created solely out of intellectual input. An author is dependent also on the individuals who feed the soul. For this, I am especially grateful to friends and family who have been there in so many constant ways and to my father, no longer living but with me still. He serves as an inspiration in my writing and thinking, continually reminding me that both activities are about finding oneself. I only hope that someday I will be sufficiently skilled to fulfill a similar role for my own children, Sarah and Joshua, who have also earned my thanks with their patience and understanding.

Finally, this book would not exist without the sensitive editing, advice, and unstinting support of Barbara Hill and Alan Rinzler at Jossey-Bass.

My heartfelt thanks to all who have nurtured me and this book.

Introduction

One of the greatest problems clinicians face today is how to respond to the concerns and conflicts that emerge at the juncture of life and death, especially those that challenge traditional healing and caring functions. Of the various issues at the meeting of medicine and mortality, perhaps none has drawn as much attention as assisted suicide. Of primary concern to the public and the courts is whether incurable and terminal patients should have the right to determine the time and manner of their own deaths, and in some cases, to end their lives with help from their physicians. To those who work with the dying, these questions are particularly pressing. If you are a physician, a nurse, or a mental health professional, you may ask yourself whether you should ever actively assist in the deliberate death or suicide of an incurable and terminal patient, or even help a person with this ultimate decision.

Although the ethics of assisted dying have been debated for centuries, the subject is no longer the exclusive concern of ethicists and theologians, and discussion of assisted suicide is no longer a social taboo. The topic is being discussed with remarkable frequency in newspapers and medical journals and has been debated before the highest courts in the land. Voters and legislators have been actively grappling with the issue for several years, and public opinion is now overwhelmingly opposed to the current legal prohibition.

Of central concern is the redefinition of the practice of medicine and the increasingly widespread expectation on the part of patients that their physicians should help them die. Some patients further expect that their psychotherapists should not prevent such acts but should support their decisions. It is now taken for granted by many health professionals, especially those working in hospices, that many incurable and terminal patients will bring up the subject.

***

The idea of assisted dying raises concerns about the very nature of medicine and therapy, about the appropriate role of clinicians, and about the inherent conflicts that may exist between saving life and alleviating suffering, between healing and harming, between intervening and respecting individual autonomy and choice. These are more than professional or intellectual dilemmas; they are also deeply personal. In considering them, you will find yourself confronting your own fundamental beliefs about living and dying, quality of life, caring, and respect for the wishes of others. The issues may also evoke personal fears—of suffering, abandonment, dependency, loss of control, and death itself. Your responses will depend greatly on your moral and religious perspectives, your spiritual concerns about suicide and the ending of human life, and conceptions of your own identity. Do you think of yourself as an invulnerable clinician or as a mortal who one day may be in a terminal condition yourself?

No longer is the request for assisted death a rarity. As one hospice medical director told me, "It's common in hospice for most of our patients to talk about assisted suicide or to request help in dying early on in the course of their hospice admission." Surveys in recent years have shown that large numbers of physicians receive explicit requests for aid in dying, and nearly one quarter of these are fulfilled. Among physicians treating AIDS patients in the San Francisco metropolitan area, more than half of those responding to a survey conducted by Slome and others had granted at least one request for assisted death.

I, too, in my work as a social psychologist, have grown accustomed to requests for aid in dying, or at least for discussion of the issue. Some requests come from those with incurable and terminal conditions, others from partners or family members of those facing the inevitability of death. Although I am used to receiving these requests, I am far from comfortable in responding to them. I will never be completely at ease discussing the issue with individuals who view assisted death as their only option, especially when they have not talked deeply with their clinicians or otherwise explored the alternatives.

More than ever, I experience a mixture of emotions. I feel tremendous compassion for these patients because of their physical and emotional suffering, their perception and fear of limited options, and the decisions they and those close to them believe they must make. I also feel empathy and concern for clinicians whose patients want to discuss ending their own lives or actually ask for help in dying, particularly when neither party knows how to proceed or how to make such a decision. In addition, I feel at times a great sense of dismay when patients or their families ignore each other's emotional needs, when a patient's intolerable pain or suffering is not acknowledged, when effective solutions for alleviating distress are not pursued by patients or their clinicians, when fearful or autonomy-driven patients stubbornly argue against any other option, and when all involved refuse even to talk with each other honestly about the subject.

I am not a physician. I take comfort in the fact that I cannot write lethal prescriptions and do not need to make decisions about helping others die. I am an academic, an educator, a researcher, and a group facilitator and counselor to the dying and their families. For a time, I also served as regional director for the Hemlock Society U.S.A., a national "right to die" organization. Over the past several years, I have worked with numerous incurably and terminally ill patients and their significant others on end-of-life decisions. I have met with or interviewed hundreds of spouses, partners, family members, and others who have participated in some way in assisted suicides. I also have had heartfelt discussions with numerous clinicians and have become aware of both their professional and their personal concerns. Like many others, I feel a sense of uncertainty because of the complexity of the issue and the pull of the conflicting forces that are often at play.

Hearing a request for assisted death is certainly not easy for anyone. I have never grown inured to such requests or to the stories that accompany them. Each represents an individual crisis, a personal battle often filled with fear and confusion. If you are like me, even a patient's desire to talk can be a difficult burden. After all, the person is not just asking for help; he or she is demanding that one look differently at one's role as a healer, reexamine one's ethical values, and perhaps step across the boundaries set by personal belief and ideas of professional practice.

Whatever your professional experience, it is likely that you have your own concerns, grounded in the daily practice of medicine or therapy. Like me, you may be troubled about how to ensure the appropriateness of an action that precipitates death. Or you may have questions about the ethics of your possible involvement at some time in the future. Underlying all of this, you may wonder how you would even begin to make such a decision and what factors you would consider.

***

If you are a physician working with incurable and terminal patients, it is likely you will face such a request. You may be unsure how to respond, verbally or practically, and you may wonder whether you should ignore the request or use it as an opportunity for further dialogue. You may be uncertain about turning to colleagues for support or opening up the dialogue to include the patient's significant others. Similarly, you may weigh whether it is a greater risk to maintain professional distance or to involve yourself emotionally. You may ask whether an obvious need for mercy should outweigh the ethics of "doing no harm," and you may ponder the personal repercussions, now and later, of agreeing to help another person end his or her life. Without legal authority to do so, you may feel that the ground rules are hazy, to say the least.

If you are a nursing professional who cares for dying patients, you may ask these same questions. Whether you work in a hospital or extended care facility, in home care, or as part of a hospice team, you too may have faced requests related to assisted death. Like many, you may be confused about what it means to hasten death. Are you already helping patients to die when you provide high-dose pain medication? Should assisted dying ever be your responsibility? You may be troubled about what to do as you hear your patients' fears related to pain, intolerable suffering, and the duration and nature of their dying process. You may see these concerns only increasing as the general population ages and as more incurable and terminal patients are cared for by nurses on the front lines of death and dying. You may be asking yourself how best to assess your feelings about the issue, how to discuss the topic with your patients and their families, and ultimately, how to make a decision about helping a person die.

If you are a mental health professional, one of whose responsibilities is the prevention of suicide, you may be increasingly confused about your role as you listen to an incurable or terminal patient express her desire to die. You may listen with uneasiness as those dealing with their own illness or that of another share their feelings about loss of dignity and diminished quality of life, emotional fatigue and despair. You may find yourself at a loss as they ask what purpose there is in continued living when they are experiencing so little joy or meaning, when their lives consist of nothing more than an endless round of medical visitations, procedures, medications, and disappointments. You may question whether you should intervene to prevent them from suiciding, even if they are incurable and terminal. Increasingly, you may feel the need to distinguish between the truly suicidal patient and a dying patient who merely wants to discuss all options. You may also ask whether there is such a thing as rational suicide, what this might actually look like, and whether a particular individual is making the right decision.

***

From my own work in this area, and from reviewing other research, I am certain that assisted deaths, although illegal and secret, are widespread. But in the absence of any willingness by professional associations to realistically address the issue, there is no certainty that patients and clinicians who follow this course of action always do so with wisdom. In the current absence of clinical practice standards, large numbers of physicians, nurses, and mental health professionals have nowhere to turn for advice. Slome and colleagues found that only 3 percent of physicians who had helped a patient die had reached out to colleagues for ideas and support. Regardless of court action or any eventual loosening of the present legal prohibition, I expect the situation to remain the same for some time to come. If anything, a loosening of restrictions might increase professional concern and confusion.

Without standards or training, most clinicians have few, if any, resources to lead them through the decision-making process. Medical and legal journals have published a handful of guidelines and some model legislation (I have even published my own), but most of this material focuses on describing the need for such a practice, determining who might qualify as a recipient, outlining how the practice might be legally controlled, and establishing safeguards against abuse. There are also "how to" manuals for the general public, one listing the most effective drugs for ending one's life.

Because of the uncertain nature of the ethical and legal status of assisted dying, nearly all writing on the subject has concentrated on the debate about whether it is ever really necessary and ethical for clinicians to participate in life-ending acts. None of the available materials take you step by step through the decision process. None help you assess your thoughts and feelings. None assist you in determining what role is best for you, how to respond in any given situation, how to talk with patients about the issue, and how you might ultimately make such a decision.

WHAT THIS BOOK WILL DO

I have written *Assisted Suicide* to provide you with the tools to answer these questions and to help you decide for yourself, as a physician or nursing professional, if and when you should give assistance to a patient who wants to die. If you are a therapist, the book is intended to help you work as effectively as possible with incurable and terminal individuals who express the same desire. Regardless of your specific role in working with the dying, this book will guide you through the complexity of the topic, the range of likely practical and emotional concerns, and an examination of your own feelings and beliefs. For physicians and nursing professionals, it also offers a step-by-step plan for the final decision process.

Throughout, I will be arguing neither for your involvement in an assisted death nor for the legalization of assisted suicide. It is not my intention to change your viewpoint. Rather, I will be arguing for wisdom in choices and decisions, and I will be providing tools to help uncover that wisdom. I will give you examples, exercises, self-assessment questions, and guidelines. Each of these elements will help you move down a decision tree toward a rational and ethical choice. My intention is to help you

- Become aware of the ethical issues and emotional and practical concerns that surround assisted dying, and think and feel more deeply about them

- Understand more clearly your own thoughts and feelings about death, dying, assisted dying, and your role as a clinician in dealing with incurable and terminally ill patients

- Grasp more precisely the meaning of a patient's expressed desire to die, or her request for your help in dying

- Expand your knowledge of the full range of concerns of patients with incurable or terminal conditions and those of their significant others

- Further your skills in listening and uncovering the most important physical and psychosocial concerns of your patient so as better to serve both her needs and yours

- Increase the quality of your interaction with patients with incurable or terminal conditions, regardless of whether they are actively considering such a decision

- Feel more comfortable about your considered position regarding assisted dying and more confident in your ability to maintain it consistently

MY POSITION ON THE ISSUE

As with any book, *Assisted Suicide* reflects the values, thoughts, and concerns of its author. These are derived from my own life experiences, work, and reflection on the subject. Although my views will become obvious in the course of the text, I feel it is important to summarize them here at the beginning.

Unlike many who take rigid positions on this issue, I must state up front that I support physician aid in dying, but with serious reservations. I believe that any assisted death should be considered an extraordinary event—one that is made available, with hesitation, to a restricted group of patients who are suffering intolerably despite the provision of the highest quality of care. At a minimum, each case must be thoroughly assessed, and the option of assisted suicide should be made available only after full discussion and exploration of the alternatives. Obviously, this position is too liberal for some and too conservative for others. Although I do not expect my view to be shared by everyone, I have great difficulty engaging with the hard-line positions on either side of the debate.

I am troubled by positions that call for continuation of the current legal prohibition, assert that assisted suicide is always morally wrong, ignore the overwhelming need of some patients for mercy, and argue that clinicians must never participate in assisted death. Such a view seemingly refuses to acknowledge that there are real patients with immense unrelievable suffering, a quality of life that is barely measurable, and a single human desire: to be able to end their own torment. I have seen far too many incurable and terminal individuals in this category, whose only options have been high-dose pain relief and terminal sedation, each of which may end personhood and also result in death. To deny the option of assisted death to these individuals is an act of callous disrespect for their humanness and a rejection of their need for mercy.

Nevertheless, I am equally troubled by positions that call for aid in dying on demand. Such positions are based solely on the principles of patient autonomy and the right to choose, and they equate assisted suicide with numerous other medical acts that hasten death, such as the refusal or withdrawal of treatment. I have seen many patients who sought aid in dying for what seemed to me the wrong reasons, and who selfishly disregarded the emotional needs of others, including their families, close friends, and clinicians. It has also become apparent to me, in talking with physicians and nurses, that there can be substantial psychic effects on clinicians who help patients die when they are not in immediate need of compassionate release.

Nothing of substance or value can come from being either overly moralistic or overly complacent on the issues involved in assisted dying. The best interests of patients, and of medicine itself, are not served either by clinicians who provide aid in dying too willingly or by those who are rigid in their refusal to even discuss the option. I believe the answer resides somewhere in the middle. Unfortunately, both sides fail to understand that the real question is how best to respond to patients in crisis, and how to turn a request for help into an opportunity to practice medicine and therapy at the highest level of quality.

A QUESTION OF MOTIVATION

I believe that the motives behind many requests for assisted death are questionable. Some appeals arise from a desire to remain autonomous and to avoid what patients anticipate will be a painful or otherwise intolerable process of dying. Although such individuals may believe that they have the "right" to end their lives, I have grave concerns, in the absence of intolerable suffering, about their involving anyone else, particularly clinicians, in this process. To do so, I believe, cheapens the value of life and transforms doctors and other health professionals into mere technicians of death.

There are other patients who may say they wish to die for reasons of autonomy or even mercy but on closer assessment may be driven by far more dubious considerations, including treatable but inadequately controlled symptoms, resolvable psychosocial issues, fear of improbable future conditions, and unrealistic worry about caregivers and financial resources. Such patients may also be suffering from depression or other psychopathologies.

I believe that cases like these can be uncovered only through careful in-depth assessment by clinicians. Such assessment takes time and is best performed by a team. It also presupposes a willingness on the part of both practitioners and patients to pursue a range of options. As long as suffering has not become intolerable, patients who lack such willingness are not only suspect but guilty of ignoring the need of clinicians to practice medicine to the best of their ability.

Beyond these two categories of patient, there are those who make thoughtful requests for assistance that may well be justifiable to most observers on the basis of the intolerable nature of their suffering and the lack of reasonable alternatives. Many patients, deprived of nearly all comfort and pleasure in life, nevertheless think carefully about their decisions and seek the opinions of their significant others before even approaching their clinicians about helping them die. Such patients often carry this approach into their discussions with clinicians, expressing a willingness to explore reasonable options as long as they can still tolerate their symptoms. For them, assisted death will be chosen only as a last resort.

THE CLINICIAN'S RESPONSE

Because of the variations just described, I believe clinicians have the ultimate responsibility for ensuring the appropriateness of any assisted death. By *clinicians*, I primarily mean physicians but also include nurses, psychiatrists, psychologists, social workers, family counselors, or other health care professionals who are somehow involved in the therapeutic care of patients.

Patients may take the lead and certainly have the right to make requests for aid in dying, but you as a clinician also have the right and the duty to respond as you see fit. Such a request transforms your relationship with the patient, and the new terms of that relationship need to be negotiated. For example, the two of you might agree that you will engage in an open dialogue, and that your own role will be to thoughtfully assess the patient's condition, provide the highest-quality response to her needs for pain control and palliative care, and fully consider her request, taking all relevant factors into account. This approach, however, requires time and effort, commodities that are not always available. I recognize this and offer this book as a blueprint to be used by a health care team.

I have concerns about the level of thoughtfulness with which a clinician might respond to a request. There are, of course, many physicians who continue to work cautiously with their patients. Instead of ignoring such an appeal, they treat it first and foremost as a call for assurance, support, and validation. They see it as an opportunity to establish closer bonds with the patient, to talk with him about his physical and emotional needs, and to respond with skill to his medical problems. This does not always lead to an agreement to help the patient die. A clinician who is open to giving such assistance may do so only in rare cases, when all else fails. For such a practitioner, quality decision making depends on an in-depth understanding of the case and sensitive responses to the particular needs of the patient.

However, I am uneasy in the knowledge that some clinicians who agree to help do so on the basis of the "physical" evidence and the motives explicitly declared by the patient. Such physicians may be highly knowledgeable of the patient's medical history and feel certain of the prognosis and degree of suffering, but they may lack knowledge of the patient as a person. As a result, they may miss important psychosocial factors that need to be considered.

Skill in diagnosing and treating illness does not always correlate with the ability to form a full human understanding of the patient or to make a wise decision about assisting in the patient's death. A good clinician is not necessarily one who agrees to help, but one who listens, learns as much as possible about the patient, explores every acceptable option, and makes certain that the circumstances and conditions are absolutely right for a decision to help.

I am troubled also by perhaps an even larger number of clinicians who refuse to discuss the topic with their patients after receiving a request. They may not know which way to turn when faced with such a demand; they may be uncertain about their own feelings on the matter or even about the factors that need to be considered in such a decision. There is also the possibility that they are strongly opposed, on principle, to the idea of assisted dying. Consequently, they may be fearful of such discussions and dismiss requests or refuse them outright. Although I understand these responses, I find myself morally outraged by them. To me, they represent the worst form of abandonment, often leaving patients and their significant relations with no other choice than to take matters into their own hands and attempt a (frequently botched) "homemade" assisted suicide. The effect can be seen in the following example.

In one case that was particularly troubling to me, an elderly woman told me of the final meeting she and her husband had had with his physician the day before he attempted to end his own life. Suffering from Parkinson's disease, soon requiring convalescent care, and facing a potential financial crisis, he had told his doctor in earlier visits about his desire to die, explained his physical and financial reasons for wanting to do so, and asked if she would give him a lethal prescription. Not only did she refuse, she changed the topic without exploring his motives or discussing alternatives.

On his final visit to his doctor, he announced that he had stockpiled some potentially lethal medications and was planning to take them the next day. The doctor's response was to say, "Good luck." His wife, who had accompanied her husband to his appointment, told me, "Upon hearing her final words, he grew very pale and quiet, and walked with even greater difficulty back to the car." She went on to say, "I was certain that he'd had a stroke." The next day, he followed through with his plan: he swallowed a small number of sedatives and, as he grew drowsy, attempted to secure a plastic bag around his head, using a rubber band. When he failed in this effort, his wife completed the task.

She told me that it was months before she realized that her husband had not had a stroke that day and that "maybe he had not really wanted to die but was merely seeking reassurance or support from his doctor that he never received. In looking back, I'm certain that he wanted his doctor and me to tell him that his life still had value. But I was in shock, suffering burnout, while his doctor could only tell him, 'Good luck.' I think her words left him no hope or choice."

***

I do not believe there is one overall position on the issue, pro or con, that works best. Rather, I feel that clinicians need to find the right solution for each patient and for themselves. What this requires is the practice of a deeper form of medicine that focuses less on medical symptoms than on the story of the whole patient.

As I will show in the following chapters, clinicians need to go in search of the patient's life circumstances, values, close relationships, religious or spiritual concerns, and sources of meaning. Without an attempt to know a patient at this deeper level, medicine is only a technical activity that focuses on the body and ignores the soul. Until clinicians can mine this deeper vein, no option—including assisted death—offers any guarantee of touching the patient as a whole person.

OVERVIEW OF THE CHAPTERS

This book is designed to lead you naturally through the process of deciding whether to help a patient die. It begins by looking at the general ethical dilemmas surrounding assisted dying and then discusses how and why patients request this option. I then suggest specific tools and dialogues that will help you understand both the expressed motives and the underlying concerns that are driving the patient's decision. The book goes on to discuss issues involving family relationships and then switches back to the clinician and the dual process of providing the highest quality of care while deciding whether to participate in an assisted death. Additional tools are described that will facilitate a close examination of your own motives. After that, the act of assisted suicide itself is discussed. Finally, the book returns to the larger social concerns from which this issue arises and provides some ideas for the future.

Chapter One begins by looking at the ethical issues that surround assisted dying. This is more than an intellectual pursuit. The intent is to help you think and *feel* more deeply about these issues, both personally and professionally. You will be advised on how to assess your own attitudes and beliefs so as to clarify your views early on about the appropriateness of assisted suicide in general.

Chapter Two introduces you to the expressed reasons why patients seek assisted dying. By means of comments from dying patients and from significant others who have participated in assisted deaths, this chapter will take you more fully into the heart of a patient's decision to die. The purpose here is to help you step outside of your own role so that you may begin to see illness, the inevitability of death, and the option of assisted suicide from the vantage points of your patients. I will show you how to develop sensitivity to even a subtle request for an assisted death, how to see what it may really represent, and how to understand the full range of physical and psychosocial motives that may underlie it.

Chapter Three provides you with tools to communicate more deeply with your patient about the decision to die. It begins by considering your response to a request, the problems of avoidance, and the risks involved in too quickly refusing or agreeing to help. Whatever your position on this topic, you will learn ways to use the patient's appeal for help and his expressed reasons as means to uncover a range of underlying issues that may be affecting his decision. This chapter also looks at the issues of rationality and depression and provides tools for assessing these factors. Throughout, dialogues and questions will prepare you to safely discuss all aspects of the clinical and human situation with your patient and to identify any symptomatic problems that may previously have been hidden.

Chapter Four addresses a wide range of issues that involve family members and significant others. It shows that if you are to become fully aware of your patient's motives and concerns, you will need to understand her connections to others. We will look at potential patient-family conflict, indicators of psychosocial and economic stressors in the home, and methods for determining possible coercion in the patient's decision. This chapter further explores the special problems that may arise when significant relations either agree or oppose the patient's desire to die. Among the topics considered are confidentiality, the inclusion of family members and significant others in the assessment process, and the implications of either ignoring or responding to the emotional needs of others as you weigh your own decision to help.

Chapter Five takes you through the initial decision-making process. Employing a care-based model, it shows how the patient's request for your help can trigger a range of clinical and personal choices. One of the tools it offers is a decision tree designed to lead you through the successive stages of decision making; this can be of use even if you staunchly oppose helping any patient die. The chapter goes on to discuss a variety of issues related to communication and provides a model for working more closely with your patient. It revisits the issue of pain and suffering and describes some clinical approaches that address these primary concerns. Finally, it looks at other end-of-life options you may want to discuss with your patient.

Chapter Six guides you through the process of reaching your final decision. It begins with an exploration of your own motives for considering the option of assisted suicide and examines, in particular, various issues related to compassion. It then addresses the problems inherent in defining another person's quality of life and in determining who might qualify for your help. Next, the chapter takes you deep within the process of assisted suicide to help you determine the durability of a request and communicate more clearly with your patient about her expectations. Finally, it addresses some problems associated with prescribing medications, the possibility of your becoming involved at the scene of the suicide attempt—which includes the potential for euthanasia—and a variety of professional and personal risks to which you may be exposed.

The Epilogue looks at some of the larger social questions that surround the issues of assisted suicide, attempts to explain the emergence of the practice at this specific time, and makes some proposals for the future.

READING WITH AN OPEN MIND

Throughout this book, my goal is to help you move beyond an academic and abstract understanding of the issues surrounding assisted dying to a clear view of your own thoughts, feelings, and concerns. Regardless of your position, I cannot stress enough the need to continue through to the end. While reading, I strongly encourage you to

- Step back from your role as a clinician and from any preconceptions you might have about the issue and about the type of patient who actively considers the option of assisted dying.

- Put aside, for the time being, any previous professional experiences you may have had with patients or colleagues who were grappling with these issues.

- Practice reversing your own attitudes and feelings and, when facing a difficult concept, place yourself in the mind of someone who holds a position contrary to your own. Try on that viewpoint and attempt to understand that person's concerns.

- Picture yourself as a patient suffering from an incurable and terminal condition. Imagine the physical discomfort, the sense of loss, the emotional confusion, and the fear for the future.

- Take on the perspective of a patient's family or significant others. Feel the impending loss, the exhaustion from caregiving, the sense of dread and incompleteness, the desire to ease your loved one's suffering as well as your own burden, and the confusion about what to do.

- Imagine, as a clinician, that you have just been asked by a patient to help him die. Ask yourself whether the words you are reading take on a different significance under this circumstance.

- Assess your own thoughts and feelings each step of the way. Note them in the margins or in a journal as you read.

- Challenge yourself throughout and constantly ask what a particular idea means to you.

*****

Reading this book is a very personal exercise. It may touch you deeply, as it deals with some of our most intimate concerns. Each of us has given thought, sustained or momentary, to dying and death. This is natural, for death is part of the human predicament. Although our personal and professional experiences with death may vary, none of us is immune to such thoughts. As individuals, we may have been personally touched or harshly gripped by loss, by the dying and death of someone close to us. We may have watched and helped care for a family member, friend, or even a partner or child, as they gradually lost their battle against an incurable and terminal illness. Moreover, as physicians, nurses, and mental health professionals, we may have had to deal with the deaths of numerous patients we knew professionally—individuals who came to us for healing, help, or advice. None of us is a stranger to the topic.

We may also have given particular thought to assisted dying. The increased role of health professionals in the modern drama of death has brought many of us face-to-face with the issues. Like me, you may crave the right to make autonomous decisions in all areas of your life but still feel uncertain about having ultimate control over your own death. You may feel even more apprehensive about such a right being extended to your patients, to say nothing of those closest to you—those you would be least willing to let go. Nevertheless, you might want to know that, given a worst-case scenario of suffering, you could expect mercy for yourself.

Our professional and personal struggles with these issues are ultimately inseparable. In looking at a terminal patient, we also see ourselves. In listening to their concerns, we often hear our own. And in receiving their requests for help, we respond both as professionals and as individuals, wondering what we would do under similar circumstances. For behind such a request are concerns that each of us has about suffering, illness, the process of dying, and death. How and where will we die? Will our dying be long and painful? Will our suffering be controlled? And will we be emotionally ready?

Throughout this book, the professional and the personal are linked. I attempt to provide you with both a very practical understanding of the professional issues and a mirror for your personal thoughts and feelings on the subject. We'll begin by looking at the ethical issues that surround assisted dying.

1

The Ethical Debate

Although the end of our lives is a certainty, there is no guarantee that our own deaths will be of our own design or to our liking. Those who look to physician-assisted dying, however, seek to change this by demanding a degree of control over the design of their deaths. Unfortunately, the type of control they seek requires the involvement of others—clinicians like yourself, who provide either emotional or therapeutic support, or who have the power to hasten death by providing lethal prescriptions or delivering medications by injection. Not only are such actions illegal in most places around the world, but they raise a number of ethical issues concerning the rights of patients, the duties of clinicians, and the effects of assisted dying on medicine as a whole and society in general.

Proponents of assisted dying focus the issue on the right of patients to make autonomous decisions and the need for mercy for patients experiencing intolerable suffering. They see little difference between "helping" a patient die, either directly or indirectly, and what occurs some six thousand times a day in the United States when deaths are managed in other ways. Most deaths in this country, they argue, are somehow planned, timed, or indirectly assisted: potentially life-prolonging treatments are often withheld or withdrawn; high-dose pain medication is given that may have the secondary effect of hastening death; and patients who are close to death may be sedated into coma while their hydration is reduced. Supporters of assisted dying also assert that it is the duty of a clinician to act as the patient's agent in alleviating suffering, even if this requires helping the patient die.

Opponents argue that under no circumstance should physicians use their medical skills to effect a patient's death, and that doing so is the same as killing. Such an act, they say, violates the integrity of physicians and the Hippocratic mandate to heal and to "do no harm." They further argue that, no matter how humane the motivation, helping patients die in this manner ultimately damages all physician-patient relationships, devalues human life, and if legally sanctioned, would have detrimental effects on society and the practice of medicine.

As with other high-profile medical and legal issues involving the end of life, from the long controversy surrounding abortion to historic court actions in *Quinlan* and *Cruzan* over the withdrawal of life-sustaining treatment, we are presently far from achieving consensus. Not only is assisted dying illegal in nearly all jurisdictions worldwide, but there has been a clear reluctance to discuss the issue in ways that acknowledge the underlying medical and human realities, seek to reduce the potential for harm, and recognize the opportunity to improve care for large numbers of interested patients.

Indeed, there are no set guidelines to help you even talk with patients about their reasons for wanting to end their lives. Similarly, there are few tools to help you consider your own beliefs, ethical values, and motivations. My aim is to remedy these deficiencies to some extent. As you will see in the following chapters, however, the tools I offer do not instantly define who is or is not qualified to receive your help. Instead, they are designed to help you think more deeply about all the relevant issues and respond more readily to the full range of a patient's concerns.

In the absence of clear and strict guidelines, I believe it imperative that the decision on assisted death be made on a case-by-case basis. I am uncomfortable with the idea of blanket categories of patients qualifying for this option. A terminal or incurable condition by itself does not seem enough. Nor does physical pain or suffering—at least, without prior attempts to ameliorate it. Criteria must be derived from the specific concerns and needs of the individual patient. Absolute solutions may be impossible to find.

Only in the Netherlands has the dilemma been resolved. Physician-assisted death has been practiced there, within guidelines and under official scrutiny, for two decades. Currently, fewer than 3 percent of all deaths in that country are assisted, mostly through euthanasia. Both assisted suicide and euthanasia became legal in Australia's Northern Territory in 1996 but were banned again six months later. Physician-assisted suicide was also authorized by voters in Oregon in 1994, but implementation was delayed by a federal court injunction, and before it could become law, the initiative was overturned by the state legislature and sent back to voters to be reconsidered on the November 1997 ballot.

Most U.S., Canadian, and British advocates of assisted suicide say the option should be restricted to mentally competent adult patients who are terminally ill. Further, if opinion polls and the actions of voters are any indication, whereas most people believe assisted suicide should be legalized, they do not support euthanasia (in which the definitive action to terminate life is taken by a practitioner). For many, euthanasia poses too great a risk and raises the specter of abuse. Nevertheless, there are those who argue that broader criteria are needed for incurable patients who are suffering intolerably. There are also some who support euthanasia for competent patients who seek death but are no longer capable of taking medications orally.

No matter how clearly distinctions are drawn or how restrictive the practice proposed, difficult issues will remain. This is because assisted dying can be interpreted as both affirming and contradicting the accepted ethical standards of existing medical practice. The arguments can therefore be bent in any number of directions.

The issues involved in helping a patient die are among the most important in medical ethics. These include the limits of mercy and autonomy, the appropriateness of ending life to alleviate suffering, the apparent conflict with the clinician's obligation to "do no harm," questions about patient competence and rationality, the potential threat to the emotionally and socially vulnerable, and the possibility that assisted suicide might lead "down a slippery slope" to euthanasia and eventually to involuntary euthanasia, ending the life of a patient without any such patient request.

Buried within these are several other issues. For example, some people argue that assisted dying is unnecessary, as pain and suffering can always be controlled by some means. Others point to lack of consistency in provision of quality pain control and symptom management for the dying. Some maintain that assisted suicide should be a right of autonomy for patients, whereas others say it ignores the clinician's right to focus solely on healing and caring.

As a result of the 1997 U.S. Supreme Court decision in *Vacco v. Quill* refusing to grant the right to physician-assisted suicide, most of these concerns must ultimately be resolved by legislatures, with the help of expert opinion. In the meantime, they confront you, the individual clinician, who must listen to patients' requests, decide whether you will help them die, and determine under what conditions this might be done.

Although assisted dying has been practiced and discussed since ancient times, the issues are much more critical today, because the act itself and the demand for its availability have become so prevalent. Your assessment of these issues will be critical to

- Understanding your own feelings and beliefs about living and dying, quality of life, the hastening of death, and patient care

- Ensuring that your work with the dying reflects the depth of your values and beliefs

- Determining how you communicate with your patients, whether you should involve their significant others, and what topics will be most important to discuss

- Influencing your thoughts and decisions about appropriate treatment, including the best response to the concerns and requests of patients

The purpose of this chapter is to help you understand the complexity of these issues and increase your self-knowledge. To achieve the best results from your reading, I would recommend the following strategies:

- Assume a nonjudgmental attitude. Let go of your assumptions and make yourself receptive to the opinions and concerns of others.

- Observe your full reaction to these issues—intellectual, professional, and emotional.

- Move beyond an intellectual understanding of the issues to responses that arise from your emotional core and spiritual beliefs.

- Imagine how you might respond to a patient's request for your assistance. Record your thoughts in a journal or in the margins of the page.

***

I will divide the ethical issues involved in assisted dying into three working categories: those that relate to the patient, those that relate to the clinician and the practice of medicine, and those that concern the rationality of a patient's request for assisted death.

In each of these areas, I will present a number of arguments that support or oppose assisted suicide. It is important to realize, however, that none of the categories can be looked at in complete isolation from the others. There is significant overlap. For example, issues relating to mercy and autonomy appear in all three categories though they are the particular focus of the first.

PATIENT-CENTERED ISSUES: AUTONOMY AND MERCY

The most common arguments in support of assisted dying rest on two basic principles of what might be termed "patient-centered" ethics: autonomy and mercy. The principle of autonomy argues that individuals have the right to make their own treatment choices, even in matters of life and death. The idea of mercy focuses on the need to prevent or alleviate suffering.

The principle of autonomy is considered to be one of the most important ethical principles in medicine. It holds that patients have a right to exercise control over most aspects of their lives and to make key choices according to their own values. When this principle conflicts with others, it almost always takes precedence. It is incorporated into laws governing medical practice and into the regulations requiring patients' informed consent to any treatment. Individuals who are competent and informed have the right to make their own medical decisions, including refusal of intervention, even for life-threatening though reversible conditions. Supporters of assisted dying argue that the principle of autonomy should be extended to many incurable and terminal patients so that they may end their lives at the time of their own choosing, with assistance from their physicians.

The principle of mercy has its source in the idea that clinicians should do all they can to relieve physical distress and do nothing to cause further pain and suffering. Treatments that cause suffering must have the purpose of returning the patient to a state of health. When a patient is incurable or terminal, and suffering intolerably, mercy requires health professionals to do all they can to alleviate that torment. At a minimum, this means providing the best pain control and palliative care. Proponents of assisted dying argue, however, that sometimes the only way to end suffering is to end the life of the sufferer. They might agree with the poet Tennyson, who said, "And sweet is death who puts an end to pain."

The question, then, is whether patients should be assured the availability of a merciful end, upon their request, in the event that their physical distress reaches a level they can no longer endure. On a more personal level, the question is whether you, as a clinician, can ever ethically support such a decision on the basis of patient autonomy or mercy or find it ethical to help such a patient end her life. We will begin by briefly looking at the notion of autonomy.

Autonomy Versus the "Good Death"

Opponents of assisted suicide, though respecting patient autonomy as one of the most important ethical principles in medicine, reject its authority when the patient's decision is to seek death. They find the decision abhorrent and believe it to be rooted in depression or mental illness or based on fear or selfishness. And it is particularly abhorrent because it asks a clinician to engage in an act of "killing." This view holds that individual rights are subordinate to societal rights, which exist to protect social values and life in general.

The opponents argue that assisted dying can never be in the best interests of a patient or a clinician. Many suicidologists, for example, suggest that assisted dying is but a form of preemptive suicide and that there is little difference between physician-assisted dying and any other suicide. It merely transfers much of the responsibility from the patient to the physician. By so doing, it gives the appearance of legitimacy to what is actually an irrational act. These critics maintain that there can be no autonomy in any choice that results in death. Autonomy requires competence and rationality, and no one rationally chooses death.

Other critics, especially those in the hospice movement, argue that the request is often but an attempt to avoid the anticipated *process* of dying. What these patients really desire is to escape from their fears of future pain and suffering, dependency, or abandonment. But these fears may be unrealistic.

Finally, some argue that assisted death is linked to a "weakness of character" and results in missed opportunities for self-knowledge, spiritual growth, and the healing of relationships—all of which can come through the dying experience. By selfishly evading this, patients fail to learn that "dying is about letting go of control." And by bringing death too soon, it prevents patients and their families from finding benefit, meaning, and value in dying. As Edmund Pellegrino states, "A good death is the last act of a drama," which assisted dying "artificially terminates before the drama is really completed."

Supporters angrily denounce such statements as "presumptuous, paternalistic, and intolerant." Opponents presume to know what is best for the patient—an attitude that violates the entire basis of autonomy. "Paternalism," Franklin Miller says in a 1995 article, "goes hand in hand with intolerance." Others argue that the idea of the "good death" reflects oppressive religious values and implies that there is but one model of death to which we must all aspire. The notion of the "last act" also suggests that the drama is not the patient's but is to be written for the satisfaction of some unnamed audience. Moreover, any knowledge or personal growth gained from the dying experience depends on what exactly is being "preempted." If a patient has endured suffering and has defined her quality of life as almost nonexistent, an assisted death may only preempt final suffering of an even more intolerable form.

Proponents further maintain that all of these arguments against assisted dying might also be applicable to deaths hastened by high-dose pain medication, the withholding or withdrawal of life-sustaining treatment, or the sedation of a patient to the point of coma. Nevertheless, no one argues against our right to refuse unwanted treatments that may prolong our lives. Moreover, sedation and high-dose morphine may not only hasten death but may diminish a patient's communicative and cognitive skills, destroying her sense of personhood as well as any ability to find meaning in the dying experience.

Merciful Acts or "Lazy" Medicine?

Another key issue is whether assisted dying is ever really necessary. Some see it as a "lazy" form of medicine and argue that nearly all pain can be controlled. Alleviation of suffering may sometimes be difficult, but it can almost always be achieved through methods of pain control and palliative care already available, especially through hospice. Although death is the ultimate end point in all care of terminal patients, the emphasis should not be on providing them with the means of suicide but on ensuring high-quality comfort care wherever possible.

Others admit that there are recognizable problems in the care of many dying patients but believe the emphasis on assisted dying is a negative response that places too much attention on failure of care. Instead of helping patients die, individual clinicians, and the profession as a whole, need to correct any deficits in patient care that currently exist. This is more appropriate than attempts to eliminate suffering by eliminating the sufferer.

Opponents further suggest that assisted dying creates a false sense of autonomy. Patients who seek assisted suicide wrongly assume this to be the best means to end their suffering. It is not. Real autonomy at life's end, in this view, can only be realized when a full range of affordable treatment options is accessible to everyone and patients fully understand them.

In response, supporters argue that the reality being missed is that vast numbers of incurable and terminal patients are presently facing pain and suffering that is not being alleviated and that many find intolerable. To deny them the option of an assisted death ignores their torment and their desires as autonomous persons. Although much more can be done to promote education on pain control and palliative care, medical institutions have been aware of the problem for at least two decades and have yet to resolve it. Meanwhile, tens of thousands move toward death each year in unrelieved agony.

There are several reasons why suffering continues. Some are institutional and can be removed only with institutional change. Others are indigenous to the nature of suffering, given our current level of medical expertise.

- Many die in hospital settings where undertreatment for pain and lack of adequate care for the dying are the norm.
- Hospices are not available to all patients who might benefit from this type of care.
- Even patients served by hospice cannot always be guaranteed a reasonable quality of life and freedom from physical torment before their deaths.
- Suffering cannot always be controlled, as it often involves several unrelenting physiological symptoms in addition to pain.

Advocates maintain that although most people die within hospital settings, vast numbers of them face severe pain and isolation. The national SUPPORT study, released in 1995, indicated that undertreatment for pain is the norm in the major institutions studied. Nearly 40 percent of seriously ill patients were found to have had severe but potentially treatable pain for several days before they died. Further, the expressed preferences of patients for end-of-life treatment were often ignored by or unknown to their physicians. More haunting is that there were no improvements even when specially trained nurses were available to act on patients' behalf as intermediaries with physicians.

The Limits of Hospice Care

Supporters also point out that although hospice care can provide many terminal patients with substantial benefits, hospices presently serve under 15 percent of the dying, even though this figure includes about 40 percent of those who die from cancer and AIDS. Many patients do not qualify for hospice. Among them are patients who live alone, lack family caregivers, or have conditions with an unpredictable prognosis. Hospice has strongly recommended, and in some instances has required, that patients be maintained through home care with the assistance of family members or other unpaid support persons capable of providing for some of the patient's needs around the clock. When this is not possible, similar services provided at long-term care facilities are often the only answer. Patients who have fought for independence all their lives may well balk at such a solution.

Currently, hospices are well adapted to their traditional population but are unable to provide optimal care for other groups of patients. For example, individuals with end-stage coronary disease or liver or renal failure are seldom served in hospice programs. Although innovations in care are now being explored, and there is increased talk of providing hospice-like services within hospital settings, these initiatives have yet to be implemented.

Moreover, even those patients served by hospice cannot necessarily be guaranteed an acceptable quality of life and freedom from physical torment before their deaths. This is readily admitted by many hospice personnel. For example, about a third of cancer patients suffer pain severe enough to require significant analgesia, usually opioid drugs, and perhaps upwards of 10 percent experience pain that cannot be controlled even with the best care available.

Beyond this, there are several physiological symptoms in addition to pain that are common to the dying process across many illnesses. Suffering can involve such symptoms as severe weakness, dizziness, or drowsiness; "air hunger," in the form of labored breathing or a struggle against suffocation; or even uncontrollable vomiting or diarrhea. As a cancer patient once told me, "Actually, pain is not a major concern—just bring on the morphine. It's everything together that makes going on like this so damn difficult." Thus suffering can be wide-ranging and entail extreme, general, unrelenting discomfort.

Although supporters of assisted suicide agree that much more can be done to aid such patients, they say that the promise of better care in the future should not mean that current patients be forced to suffer or face every indignity while they wait for death. As one woman told me, "I'm alive, but this is not living." She called her daily life "a painful death watch."

Supporters argue that the principles of mercy and autonomy demand that patients have the additional option of assisted death. However, they have disagreed on the question of whether mercy and autonomy should be given equal value or whether the autonomous desire of a patient to die should be given priority, regardless of his current level of suffering.

? Questions to Ask Yourself

The principles of autonomy and mercy provide the best starting point for an assessment of your own beliefs and feelings about assisted dying. You might start by asking yourself the following key questions:

- Do I regard assisted dying as a form of killing?
- Can I justify physician-assisted dying on any grounds? If so, do I justify it solely on the basis of patient autonomy, solely on the basis of mercy, or on the basis of both?
- Is physician-assisted dying ever really necessary? If so, under what conditions?
- Might the suffering of a patient be severe enough to justify my working with him, discussing his desires for an assisted death, and even supporting his decision to end his life?
- Might the suffering of a patient be severe enough to morally justify my providing him aid in dying?

CLINICIAN-CENTERED ISSUES

Clinician-centered ethical issues relate to the practice of medicine itself. They include concerns over the impact of assisted dying on the individual clinician, the medical profession, and society.

Allowing, Enabling, and Causing Death

An issue closely related to that of "killing" and "doing no harm" is whether assisted suicide crosses the boundary of acceptable medical practice any more than other actions that are more common and legal and that also result in the deaths of patients.

This issue focuses on what it means to allow, enable, or cause a death. Many clinicians who do not hesitate to withhold treatment from a patient with a do-not-resuscitate order often feel uneasy stopping treatment under the same circumstances. Although medical ethicists claim there is no distinction, some clinicians say there can be a psychological difference. On the other hand, surveys have shown that clinicians without such misgivings may nevertheless express reservations about providing patients with the means to die or about helping them more directly through euthanasia. Enabling or causing a patient's death is viewed as more threatening by clinicians because of their level of involvement and because the cause of death is "unnatural."

Unlike aid in dying, deaths inadvertently caused in the performance of mercy—by the double effect of morphine or by sedation to alleviate suffering—have long been accepted in medical practice. When narcotic analgesics are used competently and with the intention of reducing pain, clinicians are not held responsible when a death takes place. (This was affirmed in the Supreme Court's 1997 ruling in Vacco v. Quill.) Also accepted is allowing a patient to die by withdrawing life-sustaining treatment, an act that was once termed "passive" euthanasia. The right to stop treatment has been recognized in numerous court cases since the 1976 ruling by the New Jersey Supreme Court in the Karen Ann Quinlan case. It was upheld in the 1990 Cruzan decision by the U.S. Supreme Court.

Is There a Difference?

Opponents have long held that there is a valid distinction between assisted dying and either double effect or cessation of treatment.

They claim that assisted dying constitutes active medical intervention to cause death by unnatural means, whereas deaths from these other actions are either unintended results or are natural deaths brought about by patients' decisions.

Those who support assisted dying, however, claim that such actions are just as deliberate in hastening death, and that it is inconsistent to apply the "do no harm" rule only to assisted dying. They ask, "Does assisted dying involve any more 'harm' than a death caused by respiratory failure from morphine or from slow asphyxiation upon withdrawal of ventilation?" Although all three acts end in death, supporters claim that assisted dying is more honest. In fact, patients who request it are often more aware of the effects of this intervention, are voluntarily seeking their deaths, and are actively directing this result. Further, those who ask for such assistance may be suffering more intensely and may be far more competent than the patients in the other two groups.

This issue has come to the fore as a result of rulings by the Second and Ninth U.S. Circuit Courts, which have seen no distinction between "allowing" and "enabling" a death. The Second Circuit Court ruled in 1996 in *Quill* v. *Vacco* that a death resulting from the removal of a ventilator is "not natural in any sense," as it comes by "asphyxiation." Similarly, removal of artificially delivered fluids and nutrition cause "death by starvation" or "dehydration." If any such deaths are brought about by a patient's request, they are "nothing more nor less than assisted suicide." The court further stressed that "physicians do not fulfill the role of 'killer' . . . by prescribing drugs to hasten death any more than they do so by disconnecting life support systems." Rather, clinicians are merely enabling patients to end their lives. This was where the court saw a distinction from euthanasia, which it said "causes the death of another by direct and intentional acts." These lower court rulings were overturned in 1997 in *Vacco* v. *Quill* and *Washington* v. *Glicksberg*.

Physician-assisted suicide—or enabling patients to die—has long been seen in the United States as more palatable than euthanasia. The main reason is that it ensures that patients maintain ultimate control over their own deaths. Another advantage is that it eliminates the need for clinicians to cause death directly. Physicians can be removed from the death, both physically and psychologically, as the death can occur a day, a week, or several months after the prescription is provided. Although research on these effects has yet to be conducted, I would assume that several factors might be important here, including the physician's values, ethical beliefs, and degree of support for assisted suicide; the degree of suffering of the patient; and the patient's timing of his death. Important, too, is that with assisted suicide, the patient is under no pressure to end his life at a particular time merely because he has made an appointment with a physician.

Euthanasia can grant a merciful death to those patients who are unable to take matters into their own hands. It thus extends mercy to those who may need it the most while also allowing them to live beyond the point at which they can no longer swallow or hold down medication. Opponents, however, consider such an act far more dangerous than assisted suicide because death is placed in the clinician's hands, not the patient's. They further claim it can be more damaging to a clinician because it allows no psychological buffer in geography or time. No one has yet looked deeply at how the practice of euthanasia might affect physicians. Opponents say it may engender a growing appetite for this type of power; others counter that such an action might weigh on the physician's conscience and therefore be more difficult to repeat. Without research, all of this is conjecture.

The initial question to ask yourself as a clinician is whether such distinctions between allowing and helping matter to you. You might then ask whether there is any ethical difference between assisted suicide and euthanasia—between enabling and causing death. Do certain acts "feel" more ethical than others? Do you feel moral opposition to any acts in particular? Could you personally engage in such acts? If you have the answers to any of these questions, you are a step closer to understanding your own limits.

The Demands of Integrity

Another concern raised about assisted dying is that in violating the "do no harm" principle, medicine will forfeit its claim to be "an ethical and trustworthy profession." Opponents argue that participation in such acts might well destroy the integrity of physicians and the medical profession. They foresee a damaging psychological impact on both clinicians and patients, leading to an irreparable breakdown of trust. A patient might ask, "If my physician kills others, how can I be sure she believes my life has quality and is doing all she can to heal me?" And a physician might ask, "Why should I help this patient live, when I've helped others to die whose conditions were not as bad?" She might also think, "Maybe I should suggest assisted dying as the most advisable option in this case."

Opponents see the act of assisted dying as violating whatever trust patients currently have in medicine. One of the foundations of this trust is that clinicians are prevented from "killing" their patients. That prohibition, along with medical licenses and board certification, offers a powerful assurance of responsible practice. Helping a patient die shatters that assurance and is akin to abandonment.

Supporters retort that the primary responsibility of clinicians is to their patients, not to some public relations image of their profession. Miller and Brody, for example, have argued that there are four basic duties that characterize ethically appropriate medical practice: to practice competently; to avoid disproportionate harm to patients in providing medical benefits; to refrain from fraudulent representation of medical knowledge and skills; and to maintain fidelity to the therapeutic relationship with patients, which includes not abusing trust and not abandoning patients.

All of these duties are relevant to assisted dying. The duty to practice competently might mean that clinicians should be able to identify the beginning of the dying process and to shift from curative approaches to caring. Competence might also include providing the best pain relief and palliative care available and being able to recognize when a patient's suffering is intractable and intolerable. Avoiding disproportionate harm might mean recognizing the point at which death is less "harmful" than a life of torment. And refraining from fraudulent representation of medical knowledge might require that only competent clinicians, trained in palliative care and communication skills, be able to work with dying patients or help them die.

Supporters often see the most important of the four duties to be maintaining fidelity to the therapeutic relationship. In voluntarily requested assisted death, Miller and Brody, for example, see the clinician as the patient's agent, "not as the arbiter of death." She may help the patient die, but only after working closely with him and attempting by expert means to reduce the harm caused by suffering.

Fidelity also includes the duty not to abuse trust and not to abandon patients. Supporters argue that "trust" demands not that the clinician never help a patient die, but that she follow through on a decision made by the patient and agreed to by the clinician after competent input and discussion of alternatives. Some claim that ultimate trust can exist only when patients know that their physicians will compassionately help them die, at their reasoned request, should other efforts fail to alleviate their physical distress.

As for abandonment, some advocates maintain that the ultimate abandonment is the refusal of clinicians to help patients fulfill their decisions about life and death in the face of intolerable suffering.

Questions to Ask Yourself

As a clinician, the questions to ask yourself are how best to maintain your patient's trust and how to act with integrity in caring for him throughout the dying process. How can you assure a patient that you will work in his best interest and adhere to the fundamental principles that govern ethically appropriate medical practice? You might begin by asking yourself the following questions:

- Do I promote trust by opening or by closing communication on the subject of assisted dying?
- Could anything that I say or do be interpreted by my patient as a form of abandonment?
- Do I stimulate trust or distrust when I agree (or refuse) to consider the possibility of helping my patient die?
- Am I abandoning a patient if I refuse (or agree) to help him die?
- In attempting to address patients' concerns about pain and suffering, do I work with skill, patience, and the best medical knowledge?

The Slippery Slope

The bioethicist Thomas Beauchamp has stated that rules against killing "are not isolated moral principles" but "pieces of a web of rules" that form our moral code. "The more threads one removes, the weaker the fabric becomes." This is the crux of what has been termed the slippery slope argument against assisted dying. If the practice is allowed, runs the argument, the boundaries will expand beyond a restricted set of patients to ever larger populations. Assisted suicide for the terminally ill will in due time lead to euthanasia for the incurably ill—even without their request.

Daniel Callahan, in a 1992 article, warns, "What begins as a right of doctors to kill under specified conditions will soon become a duty to kill." And Leon Kass asks, "Do you want your doctor deciding, on the basis of his own private views, when you still deserve to live and when you now deserve to die?"

The fear is that even the most conscientious physicians may need protection from their own temptations to rid themselves of troublesome failures under their care. Laws prohibiting assisted death are seen as the best protection against this. Kass quotes a hospice physician as saying, "Only because I knew that I could not and would not kill my patients was I able to enter most fully and intimately into caring for them as they lay dying."

Callahan has said that helping patients die—even at their own request—allows physicians "to accept the conceit that nature has now fallen wholly within the realm of human control." Clinicians who kill, with or without legal authority, break down social values and desensitize themselves to the importance of life.

Vulnerable populations, like the poor or the elderly, are especially at risk, for assisted dying will quickly become financially driven. Economic pressures may well create variations in health care delivery and eventual rationing of services, leaving assisted death the only choice for those patients considered "unsalvageable" by their managed care corporations. As one opponent said, "If every person with a terminal illness could be a potential candidate for assisted suicide, a fatal prescription could become a powerful cost-control tool."

In addition, psychological pressures may make it difficult for emotionally vulnerable populations—the helpless and seriously ill—to avoid the influence or coercion of others. Kass suggests that "we might then also sweep up some who do not really want to die, but who feel they should not live on, because to do so would be selfish or cowardly" in the face of this less expensive alternative. Callahan's earlier comment about physicians might thus become applicable to patients: what begins as a right to die under specified conditions may soon become a duty. An autonomy model of health care, based on multiple options, may be undermined by a cultural expectation that assisted dying is the most appropriate way to depart from life.

Supporters describe as brutal this vision of a society and medical profession without compassion, indifferent to the abuse of the vulnerable. It assumes that physicians will readily become technicians without conscience, acting willingly against patients and the long-standing tradition of medicine. Those in favor of assisted suicide point out that doomsayers made similar predictions about the

practice of stopping treatment, yet none of the grim scenarios outlined then have been realized, even though that practice carries a
higher potential for abuse. They ask if it is right to deny mercy to
patients who are suffering and dying today in order to prevent some
unnamed abuse from occurring to unknown patients at some questionable time in the future.

They argue that such "slippery slope" arguments lack clarity.
Where would the impetus for the "slide" come from? Courts extending or reducing individuals' rights? Legislatures enacting cost-
containment measures? Greedy HMOs restricting health benefits?
None of this is spelled out. The predictions of general ethical collapse ignore the power of the voting public, legislators, and physicians to act for the public good. They also disregard the compassion
with which families seek the best care for dying parents, children,
and siblings, and the power of the marketplace to improve care for
the dying by advancing hospice as a less costly alternative to treatment in hospitals.

As regards desensitization to the value of human life, supporters argue that this may already be present in clinicians who ignore
or dismiss too quickly the requests of patients for aid in dying. They
argue that clinicians become calloused not necessarily by helping
patients die but by failing to validate their concerns and by taking
control away from them in their end-of-life decisions.

As evidence, they point to current practices of withdrawing
treatment and to several studies that have shown that large per-
centages of critical care physicians discontinued life-sustaining
treatment without the knowledge or formal consent of the patient
or a family member. Although such actions did not necessarily constitute abuse, and the reasons given for them were usually valid (for
example, "Further efforts would not extend a patient's life for more
than a few hours"), it is clear from these findings that clinicians
often assert authority and bring their own values into life-and-death
decisions despite the principle of patient autonomy. Assisted dying,
by contrast, returns this authority to patients, where it belongs.
Turning power back to patients might teach clinicians humility,

compassion, and the value of life—as that life is defined by each patient.

Questions to Ask Yourself

The slippery slope argument speaks to the power involved in ending life and the enormous responsibility and burden this entails. It raises questions about appropriate criteria for qualification of patients, the maintenance of boundaries, and possible effects of helping patients die. Some of these concerns are addressed in the following questions:

- Is it ever appropriate for me to assert authority in life-and-death matters, despite the principle of patient autonomy?

- Has the practice of medicine desensitized me to the value of human life? Would my helping a patient die further affect my valuation of life?

- Would legal permission to help patients die change my current behavior toward them? How? Might it increase the likelihood that I would assist a patient in this way?

- Might helping a patient die have a psychological impact on the way I practice medicine? Might it prevent me from working as effectively with other patients who have similar conditions?

- Might assisting one patient increase my willingness to help others in a similar manner?

- Might the availability of assisted death increase the potential for coercion of emotionally vulnerable populations?

- Might assisted death someday become the prevailing cultural expectation? What factors might bring this about?

ISSUES OF RATIONALITY AND VOLUNTARINESS

The third and final group of issues concerns the ability of patients to make rational, competent, autonomous decisions about ending their lives. It is one thing for you, as a clinician, to arrive at a reasoned position on helping a patient die, taking into account that individual's physical condition and level of suffering. It is another thing to be certain that the patient's request is competent, rational, and voluntary. Although I have placed these issues last, they should actually be the starting point in any consideration of a specific case.

Of particular concern is how to effectively respond to a patient's desire to end her life. Interventionists often claim that the expression of such a desire is a "cry for help" that cannot ethically be ignored. They maintain that such requests are rooted in depression or some other mental illness, or in the consequences of the incurable condition itself, which can affect cognitive functioning. They argue that instead of helping patients die, clinicians need to ensure the best pain relief and palliative care, and if necessary, intervene to prevent suicide. To ignore the patient's concerns might result in harm, negligently violate the standards of care, and constitute malpractice—breach of the duty to act responsibly to protect a patient's life from known harm.

Standards of care, argue the interventionists, demand that once the risk of suicide is foreseen, reasonable action be taken to prevent it. In this view, all potential suicides should be prevented, regardless of the physical health of the patient. Some say the intervention may go as far as involuntary commitment.

On the other side, the possibility of rational suicide in patients with terminal conditions has gained recognition over recent years, especially as a result of patients' demands, changes in public opinion toward assisted death, and the influence of the right-to-die movement, state ballot initiatives, court challenges, and the AIDS crisis.

In line with these changes, the National Association of Social Workers has come to acknowledge the right of terminally ill patients to request and receive aid in dying, under appropriate circumstances and after counseling. A 1994 policy statement said, "NASW's position concerning end-of-life decisions is based on the principle of client self-determination. Choice should be intrinsic to all aspects of life and death . . . after being informed of all options and consequences." More than accepting this right, the policy statement went on to suggest the appropriateness of social workers being present during assisted deaths. This position is in strong contrast to the traditional view that all suicides imply the presence of mental illness.

Can an Assisted Suicide Be Rational?

Traditionally, mental health professionals have denied the concept of rational suicide. Some have vehemently argued that no decision to end one's life can ever be rational, even in the case of a terminal illness. In their view, *rational suicide* is an oxymoron and, as Herbert Hendin, of the American Suicide Foundation, has said, "must be either irrational or a product of mental illness."

Opponents of assisted suicide point to studies that show the prevalence of untreated depression among the terminally ill and the relationships between pain and depression and between depression and suicidal ideation. They claim that when pain is adequately treated, both depression and suicidal ideation diminish. They add that individuals in good health may be capable of making objective judgments about assisted death, but patients with serious illnesses and unresolved symptoms are not.

According to Kathleen Foley, testifying in 1996 before Congress, competence and rationality in such cases are always doubtful, because of a complex interrelationship of psychological, existential, and physiological factors. Moreover, these factors affect not only the terminally ill patients themselves but also their families and professional caregivers, in what becomes a spiral of distress. Foley states that "the perceived distress in any one of these groups amplifies the distress of the others." The resulting anxiety and depression can, in turn, erode competence and rationality. This progression can be reversed by compassion, pain relief, and forms of palliative care available within hospice. However, hospice is not available to most dying patients.

In response, advocates of assisted dying maintain that a request for assisted death is not incompatible with mental competence, rationality, and voluntariness. The overwhelming majority of mental health professionals, according to surveys conducted by James Werth and Barbara Liddle, believe that individuals can make rational decisions to control the time and manner of their own deaths, especially when several criteria are met: an unremitting, hopeless condition; motives understandable to the mental health care professionals; a realistic assessment of the situation by the patient; and a sound decision-making process free of external coercion. Sound decision making includes consideration of all options and their potential impact on others, nonimpulsive action congruent with the patient's values, and consultation with others.

Further, although suicidal ideation is in certain instances linked to depression, it does not follow that most requests for assisted suicide are the result of impaired mental judgment. Such an idea is paternalistic in the extreme, assumes its own conclusion, and conveniently ignores the legally available and frequently exercised option of discontinuing medical treatment—a decision that can also result in death. Moreover, discounting the rationality of such requests ignores shifting cultural attitudes and majority public opinion supportive of assisted dying for the terminally ill.

Though the correlation between suicide and mental illness may hold for the general population, it does not necessarily apply in the case of terminally ill patients. Advocates look skeptically at the research that has linked suicide among the terminally ill with mental illness. Whereas most of the deaths studied in such research have been drawn from official records of suicides, many assisted suicides are secret and are reported as deaths by natural causes. These may be more rational than the publicly known suicides; at the very least, two distinct populations may be involved. Studies linking *requests* for assisted death and mental illness are similarly suspect, as they typically focus on hospital settings. My own research indicates that most such requests are made privately to personal physicians and go unreported. In such cases, either assistance is provided and covered up or the request goes unreported because the clinician does not consider it to be irrational, suggestive of pathological suicidal ideation, or cause for intervention.

Can an Assisted Suicide Be Voluntary?

Opponents of assisted suicide also frequently question whether autonomy is possible, especially when one is terminally ill, given the effects of medication and the influences of a patient's familial, cultural, and social environments. They claim there is a strong potential for exertion of undue influence and coercion by significant others, including clinicians, who may be too supportive of a patient's expressed desire for assisted death.

Worse yet, patients who are especially vulnerable during an illness, and who may already perceive themselves as burdens on their families, may feel obligated to follow others' suggestions that they should consider an assisted death. Opponents further argue that any openness in discussing the topic will only set the stage for coercion by significant others, and that autonomy may soon give way to the perceived duty of a patient to choose assisted suicide for the sake of others.

Advocates of assisted suicide argue that problematic issues concerning autonomy, competence, and possible coercion exist only because of the illegality of the practice in most areas of the world. They will continue to exist as long as professional associations vehemently oppose legal change and are unwilling even to discuss these concerns with their membership. Legalization would allow for development of strict criteria and standards for clinical practice, which would effectively eliminate the concerns.

The development of such criteria could help clinicians determine how best to work with patients, and what factors and methods to consider in patient evaluation. Criteria might also guide clinicians in assessing—with the help of mental health professionals—the influence of psychosocial factors on a patient's decision.

Clinicians might look for evidence of coercion by carefully probing a patient's motives and allowing full discussion of his concerns. Mental health professionals can be invaluable here and might look for prior evidence of mental illness, depression, suicidal ideation, substance abuse, and even the side effects of medications. They could also counsel patients and assist them in discussing and even coping with issues such as pain, suffering, depression, financial stress, and the possible effectiveness of available treatment. None of these clinical guidelines, however, presently exist.

By declaring all suicides by the terminally ill to be irrational, incompetent, or involuntary, opponents effectively close the door on productive discussion between patients and professionals. Rather than saving lives, this stance may well be resulting in the suicide of patients who could otherwise have been screened out and provided counseling and appropriate treatment alternatives.

Questions to Ask Yourself

Many clinicians remain confused about whether it is ever ethical to help patients die, to work with them on this decision, or even to talk with them about their desires. And at the center of these concerns is whether any suicide—even an assisted death in the case of a terminal illness—can be rational, competent, and voluntary.

These critical concerns are intimately linked to the ethical issues previously discussed. For example, how can a clinician work as a "patient's agent" and help that patient die if the individual's decision is irrational or involuntary? What does the assisted death of such a patient mean in the context of the slippery slope argument? What does it say about trust and integrity, "lazy" medicine, or the difference—if there is one—between enabling and causing a death? Again, you would do well to assess your own beliefs and feelings about these issues. The following questions may help you do so:

- Can a request for assisted dying ever be rational? If so, am I professionally capable to make such a determination?

- Is it appropriate for a clinician to help a patient die without the absolute certainty that her request is rational and voluntary? If not, how might I achieve the competence to make such a determination?

- Are all requests for assisted death "cries for help," and is assisted death merely another form of suicide? If so, is it appropriate or inappropriate for me to discuss the possibility of such an act with a patient, given the risks?

- Is intervention, involuntary commitment, or refusal by a clinician to discuss assisted death a form of abandonment? Might this increase the risk of actual suicide?

A FINAL EXERCISE

With the increasing professionalization of death, clinicians are forced to grapple with all the dilemmas of assisted suicide we have examined: talking versus ignoring or intervening, healing versus caring, helping versus refusing. As I have attempted to show, the place to begin is within yourself. Try first to understand your own ethical values and beliefs concerning this practice. Only by beginning to draw your own boundaries can you prepare yourself for the subtle challenges that will confront you as you meet your patients at their own crossroads.

To aid you in this task, I have designed a decision tree on ethics (Figure 1.1) that covers a few of the key issues discussed in this chapter. As you will see in reviewing the diagram, regardless of your ethical position and whether you generally support or oppose assisted suicide, you face the task of learning more about your patient, his request for your help in dying, and his underlying needs and concerns. The only way to accomplish this is to be completely open and nonjudgmental in discussing the topic and to work closely with the person to address his complaints and fears while providing the highest quality of care. I will be covering these points in the next several chapters.

FIGURE 1.1 Ethical Decision Tree.

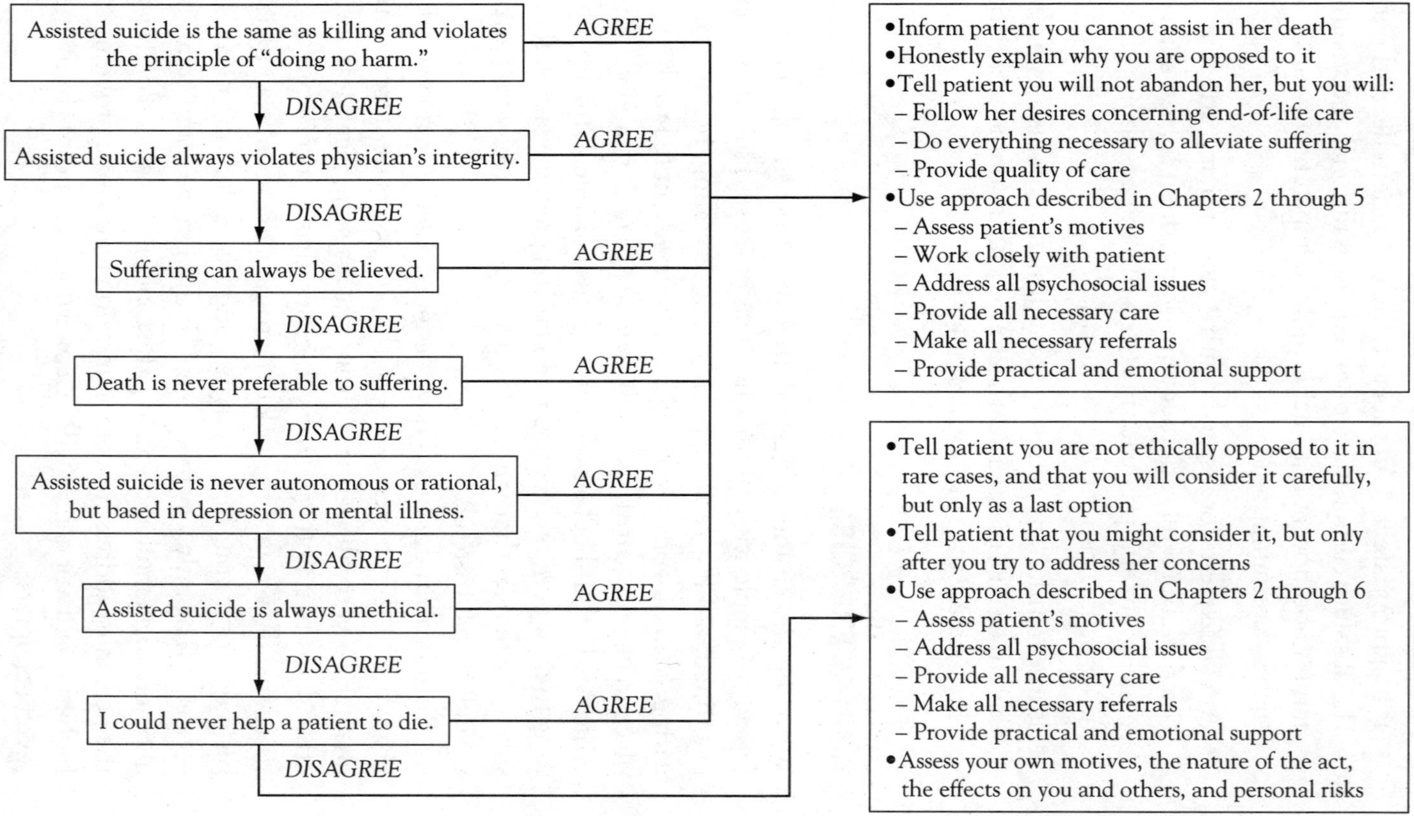

Assisted suicide is the same as killing and violates the principle of "doing no harm."

— AGREE

Assisted suicide always violates physician's integrity.

— AGREE

Suffering can always be relieved.

— AGREE

Death is never preferable to suffering.

— AGREE

Assisted suicide is never autonomous or rational, but based in depression or mental illness.

— AGREE

Assisted suicide is always unethical.

— AGREE

I could never help a patient to die.

— AGREE

DISAGREE → DISAGREE → DISAGREE → DISAGREE → DISAGREE → DISAGREE → DISAGREE

- Inform patient you cannot assist in her death
- Honestly explain why you are opposed to it
- Tell patient you will not abandon her, but you will:
  – Follow her desires concerning end-of-life care
  – Do everything necessary to alleviate suffering
  – Provide quality of care
- Use approach described in Chapters 2 through 5
  – Assess patient's motives
  – Work closely with patient
  – Address all psychosocial issues
  – Provide all necessary care
  – Make all necessary referrals
  – Provide practical and emotional support

- Tell patient you are not ethically opposed to it in rare cases, and that you will consider it carefully, but only as a last option
- Tell patient that you might consider it, but only after you try to address her concerns
- Use approach described in Chapters 2 through 6
  – Assess patient's motives
  – Address all psychosocial issues
  – Provide all necessary care
  – Make all necessary referrals
  – Provide practical and emotional support
  – Assess your own motives, the nature of the act, the effects on you and others, and personal risks

***

Whether we admit it or not, at the heart of the debate over assisted dying are concerns each of us has about illness and death. They arise from our shared experience of living and dying in an age of medical technology. You may wonder what your own illness and dying process will be like, how and where you will die, if your own final illness will be long and painful, if you will be able to tolerate pain and suffering, if you will receive quality care, and if your suffering can be controlled. You also may be anxious about whether you will burden others.

Underlying your thoughts about autonomy, mercy, and quality of care are experiences you may have had with the deaths of people close to you, including patients. Also important may be your concerns about the appropriate role of health professionals, about their power and integrity, and about the rights of patients and the possible limits to such rights. Your position on these issues may reflect the ideas you hold about the type of society in which we should live and your attitudes toward the appropriate role of clinicians and the profession of medicine itself.

The issues explored in this chapter are therefore deeply personal and may take on varying colorations, depending on your basic philosophy and religious beliefs and your immediate status as a patient, caregiver, significant other, or clinician. As a patient, you may want the right to decide but may also fear the possibility of having no other option than assisted suicide; or you may feel uncertain about how much power is safe to place in the hands of your clinicians. As a significant other, you may want all options available but feel uneasy extending rights to other concerned parties or loved ones who might act without warning. As a clinician, you may perceive the need for mercy but desire to focus on healing and be morally opposed to inducing death. Or as a therapist, you may want to prevent unnecessary suicides but also want to help others in acting responsibly in any decision, even one for assisted death.

Some of the issues I have discussed in this chapter are revisited, in different contexts, throughout the book. In the following chapter, we will look again at such issues as mercy, autonomy, and voluntariness as we hear from patients, look at their expressed reasons for seeking assisted suicide, assess their underlying concerns, and more fully examine factors that may affect their decisions.

2

When a Patient Says "I Want to Die"

Any potential act of assisted death begins with a patient's comment, a subtle statement, or a request: "Please help me die." These are not easy words to hear. They convey the ultimate dissatisfaction that a patient can express concerning her illness, treatment, and even your work as a clinician. As a result, your first response may be to dismiss the statement entirely and view it as a manifestation of temporary disappointment, exhaustion, or depression. To do so is a mistake, for such a request is not easy for a patient to make. If you respond with understanding, you create a unique opportunity to practice medicine at the highest level, to delve below the surface, to fully assess this person's concerns, and to respond to the whole patient.

Whatever form a request takes, it carries more than just an appeal for aid in dying. The words represent the culmination of this person's experience in the world. They carry her entire history—everything she has accomplished, the hopes she possessed, experiences with family, and disappointments and losses in all areas of life. They also contain her personal values, feelings about the quality of her life, attitudes toward death and suicide, and whatever spiritual beliefs she may have.

Further, these words carry a history of the patient's body and convey the sum total of her experience with illness. Such a request embraces the full record of her treatment—the diagnostic procedures, surgical interventions, and therapies she has gone through and the encounters she has had with numerous health professionals. Her words distill the range of symptoms she has endured, her confrontations with discomfort, her conversations with significant others, and her emotional responses to illness. The request for assisted dying represents far more than the desire to end one's life.

Either to accede at once to a request or to reject it outright, without delving beneath its various layers, does a disservice to the patient by treating her, in the former case, as a set of symptoms to be addressed or, in the latter, as a complex of fears to be dismissed. To respond in either way fails to recognize the depth of her communication. Both approaches deny the personhood of the patient and flout the principle that medicine treats both body and spirit.

Regardless of how you stand on this issue, you will best serve the needs of your patients by learning as much as you can about their concerns and by doing everything possible to keep the lines of communication open. Before you make any decision, I suggest listening, probing, and seeking to fully understand what a request for help actually means. In this chapter, I will be providing you with the first set of tools for accomplishing this task.

RECOGNIZING AND UNDERSTANDING REQUESTS

Requests for aid in dying, whether subtle or direct, may seem to vary very little, but each request is unique in terms of its motivation and the patient's hopes. There is no one reason why patients seek aid in dying. Rather, there are many driving forces that combine in varying ways. Although many patients desire death at the earliest possible moment, others seek the insurance they believe a lethal prescription can provide—the guarantee of escape should they need it. Then there are those who come to you with other needs; they may, for example, be seeking honesty, validation, or emotional support.

Some may approach you thoughtfully and rationally, at peace with their decision to release themselves from intolerable suffering in what they see as the only way open to them. Others may be physically exhausted and emotionally numbed from their struggle with the seemingly unending misery of an incurable condition. Then there are those who are anguished by the knowledge of what may come to pass—or fearful of what they do not know. And for others, the torment may reside in a sense of despair that their lives no longer have meaning and that continuing to live serves no purpose. There are patients who will express their concerns to you fully, and there are those who will hide their real motivations.

A request for assisted suicide cannot be answered with a simple yes or no. Rather, it is a dilemma to be investigated, whatever your position on the issue and regardless of whether you could ever help a patient in this manner. The first set of questions to be asked is

- What concerns are driving this person's desire for death?
- How might I learn more about these factors?
- If I uncover these concerns, can I help address them?

But before making a final decision to support or deny a person's request for help, it is vital to take time to understand the patient at the deepest level possible. To do this, you must

- Learn to recognize the various forms that requests for aid in dying may take
- Appreciate what a request and its possible fulfillment mean to the patient
- Understand clearly the individual's expressed motives in asking for your help in dying
- Grasp the deepest underlying rationale for this person's request to die

The Thought That Precedes a Request

You can assume that patients who ask for your help in dying have thought about it seriously for some time. If my own research and work with the dying is any indication, those who arrive at this point most often do so only after a long period of self-dialogue and reflection.

During this process, a patient's thoughts about assisted suicide may be linked to a number of existential, ethical, and practical concerns. Like many of us in periods of crisis, a patient in the throes of a life-threatening illness may consider a number of questions about the meaning and value of life, his significance in the scheme of things, and whether there is yet a purpose for him to fulfill. He may reflect on his accomplishments and failures, the value of continued suffering, the morality of assisted death in his specific circumstances, the congruence of such an act with his values, and the effects of this action on partners, family members, and others. He also may think about prioritizing and completing life tasks, about the timing of his death, and about how to recognize with certainty that the right moment has come. A person may ask himself:

- Am I in charge of my own life and death, and is this my choice to make?
- Is it wrong, and the same as suicide, to end my life if I am suffering?
- Should I share my thoughts with others and tell my family how I feel?
- Is it wrong to involve others in my death, and should I ask my doctor for help?

The importance of this self-dialogue cannot be overstated. However, not every patient thinking about assisted death asks the same questions and at the same depth. Some have a more intellectual style and attempt to find a logical answer to their dilemma. Others focus on emotional or spiritual questions.

The style of a patient's self-dialogue can also vary from moment to moment and from day to day. One day a patient might say to herself, with great emotion, "I can't live with this" or "I won't be able to follow this till the end." This would reflect her frustration and sadness at her physical condition and life circumstance. On another day, she might use the identical words, but this time they would express her pragmatic understanding of her weakness or her intolerance of pain, illness, or personal change. "I can't live with this" is then a statement of fact. It reflects the patient's self-knowledge, her awareness of her personal values and past choices, and the importance she attaches to autonomy and self-control.

An inner dialogue of this form is normal and not necessarily driven by underlying depression or mental illness. It can be part of a larger search for alternatives, part of a natural process in which the patient redefines herself as being on a path that may lead to death. As a result of this reflective process, she may come to accept her life-threatening illness, establish a new set of priorities for the brief time that remains to her, and even find a new sense of spirituality.

When a patient finally puts these ideas into words and requests your help in dying, it does not mean that the inner dialogue has ended. From what I have seen, even those who most vehemently assert their "right to die" continue this dialogue, this weighing of life and death. It continues until the patient ends her life—with or without assistance—or until time runs out and the patient dies from natural causes.

Overt and Covert Requests

Most appeals for aid in dying are immediately recognizable for what they are: a request for a prescription that could be used by the patient to hasten death or a plea for more direct action by you to end this person's life. The patient may simply say, "I want you to help me die" or "I need you to give me a prescription to end my life." Others ask, "I don't want to go through this—can you help me in some way?" Some may even candidly ask you for a specific medication, saying, "This is what I need, and I'd appreciate your help."

In a slightly less direct approach, a person may comment, "I've put up with this for too long. I really want to get this over with." Or they may ask, "Isn't there something I could take to get this over with quickly?" The intent of such statements is usually clear, and they require some response on your part.

But some requests may be less recognizable. A patient may utter words that merely hint at his real intent—for example, "I'm tired of all this" or "I don't want to continue suffering much longer." In such cases, the meaning of the communication is ambiguous and may become clear only over time, as the patient responds to your questioning with progressively less cryptic statements. The original words thus set the stage for a conversational game that requires a willingness on your part to probe for the true intent.

Patients make use of such cryptic statements because they are not as threatening as direct requests for help yet can be just as effective over time. You cannot let a remark like "I don't want to continue suffering" pass without comment. At a minimum, it serves as a conversational opener that notifies you of the patient's general level of dissatisfaction. This approach also enables a person to safely test the waters before committing himself to a more direct plea for help. It leaves a door open for escape, for saving face, should you be unresponsive to the comment.

Finally, you should be aware of other patients who may be far less candid, masking their dissatisfaction and doing their best to hide their intentions. For instance, they may complain about having difficulty sleeping and request barbiturates or other potentially lethal medications that they have read about in books or articles on suicide. Such literature has long been available from certain "right to die" organizations, and procedures are also described in detail in Derek Humphry's best-selling "suicide manual," *Final Exit*.

There are patients who view this as the safest approach, in that they do not need to admit their plans to you, discuss their reasons for wanting to die, or face the possibility of rejection. They also do not have to deal with recommendations that you might make for treatment alternatives, hospice care, crisis intervention, or counseling. Moreover, in their eyes, this covert method protects you from the legal and emotional dangers of knowing what they intend.

Whatever the degree of subtlety in a patient's remarks, you would do well to consider any statement similar to those discussed above as reason for concern and as a potential request for your assistance. It should not be ignored or dismissed.

In the following chapter, I will suggest some possible responses.

The Struggle to Make a Request

It is important to realize that patients who approach you with thoughts about assisted dying typically do so with great effort. It is no easy task for a patient to ask you to step outside your role as healer to engage in the potentially criminal act of helping her die. Similarly, it is not easy for a client in therapy to share such concerns with her therapist, when the therapist's conventional duty is to prevent suicide in all instances—even when a patient is terminal and suffering intolerably.

Some of these difficulties can be heard in the comments of a woman with whom I talked several weeks before her death from breast cancer:

> I waited for the right moment to say what I wanted, but it never seemed to come. I needed to feel absolutely comfortable, but I was worried about offending my doctor. She'd done so much for me, and had really become more of a friend. She'd been so supportive, I didn't want her to feel uneasy, or feel I was forcing her to do something out of friendship. Also, I didn't want her to think I was ready to give up, which I wasn't, or that I was saying she was a failure. This wasn't about her. She'd done her best. It was about me, and what I needed. But I didn't know how to get this across.

She saw other risks in expressing her desire. Her pain medication was no longer effective, and she knew she would soon need something stronger. She was worried that her request for a lethal prescription might jeopardize her chances of getting the treatment she needed.

I didn't think it would be a problem . . . but I didn't know for sure. With someone else, I really would've worried that they'd think I was a suicide risk, and was trying to get stronger medication just to kill myself. Although I trusted her, I wasn't absolutely certain.

This is not an idle concern. Clinicians do need to worry that their patients may use certain medications for the wrong reasons. Some patients know this and feel anxious that a request for aid in dying might result in a worsening of care, in a possible reduction in the availability of medications that are absolutely necessary for the symptoms they already find intolerable.

Similarly, some patients fear that a request might be heard as an absolute statement of a desire to die, whereas what they are really seeking is "insurance" against worse suffering. Other patients express the concern that a request might redefine them as "bad" patients and subject them to neglect or abandonment. Although many of these fears are groundless, they are understandable given that so many incurable patients do feel forgotten by their clinicians. The medical literature is filled with reports describing the difficulties some physicians have in working with the dying. For many, a patient's death signifies failure—to say nothing of the reminder it offers of their own mortality—and they prefer to focus their efforts on those whom they can still help.

Thus patients' fears about the effects of a request are not necessarily irrational. The possibility of withdrawal by health professionals is not out of the question. Even if a clinician would not consciously respond in this manner, some patients are anxious that he might not feel as comfortable treating them, or be as responsive to their needs, after being asked to help them die. As a woman in a discussion group told me:

I kept thinking, "Am I taking an unnecessary risk here?" I know I've been lucky getting good care, and this made me feel guilty. On top of it all, I wasn't sure this was something I'd ever do. So I thought, "Here I am with a great doctor, somebody who really cares. I shouldn't upset the cart."

WHAT A REQUEST REALLY REPRESENTS

Those who request aid in dying can be categorized in a number of ways. For example, they may vary in terms of how certain they are about their decision and in terms of when they plan to carry out such an act.

Some patients are more certain of their decision than others and are seeking more immediate relief. These include individuals who are suffering the intolerable effects of a life-threatening illness or degenerative condition and have already made the decision to end their lives sometime in the near future. Some may have believed in assisted suicide for years, as a matter of personal philosophy; others may have been recently converted to the idea by their own experience of grave illness.

Patients who have made a firm decision to end their lives are not the only ones who might ask for your help. There are others who may simply be exploring the full range of alternatives, including assisted suicide, in preparation for a worst-case outcome. In my own experience, this group constitutes the majority of patients who request aid in dying. A hospice medical director told me:

> They commonly ask our nurses once they trust them enough. They say, "I've stockpiled medications," or they ask for medications to stockpile and say, "I have cancer of the pancreas, and I don't want to go through this, and I want you to help me, or at least, I don't want you to interfere."
>
> And the nurses commonly bring it to the team meeting, but we've gotten to the point where we don't talk about it much any more. They just respond to the person, saying "Well, let's just both do our best here for a while and see what happens."
>
> We rarely see those folks follow through on their original request or intent to kill themselves. I'm convinced that the requests and expressions of intent far outnumber the people who wind up doing it or who wind up in a place where they really have to do it.

Finally, there are those who may bring up the topic and request your help for purposes other than actually obtaining a prescription. They are looking for some other form of "medicine"—honesty, truth, validation, emotional support, personal power, or a willing ear. Patients may request aid in dying for the purposes of

- Obtaining an honest assessment of the seriousness of their condition
- Eliciting a hopeful prognosis
- Further mobilizing resources and the talents of clinicians on their behalf
- Demonstrating their discontent with their illness and treatment and convincing others of the absolute misery and despair they feel
- Securing proof that others are listening
- Winning reassurance that their lives still have value
- Evoking positive emotional responses (sympathy, concern) from the clinician

Unless you know a patient extremely well, you may not be immediately certain of his intent. This is all to the good, as it necessitates that you undertake a deep exploration. By now, the benefits of such work should be quite apparent. An in-depth assessment of a patient's motives can reveal unmet treatment concerns that you can then attempt to address. Obviously, such an assessment can also provide information that will assist you in deciding if and when you should help the patient die.

WHAT THE PROMISE OF HELP CAN REPRESENT

A prescription or a clinician's promise of an IV overdose may have a range of special meanings for the patient. Just as a request can represent more than a desire to die, so access to a prescription has broader significance. Although the overt purpose of the prescription is to provide the means of suicide, it also can be insurance against intolerable suffering, a weapon against powerlessness, a tool by which the patient can control his final destiny, and a guarantee that he has the ultimate right to choose. One man told me:

> This is more than a drug. It's like an open-ended airline ticket I can use should it all become just too much for me. Now that I have it, it doesn't mean I'm going to use it. That day may never come.

For many patients, the prescription or promise can also trigger a change in the way they view their relationship with you. They have gained power by becoming partners in their health care choices and by assuming ultimate responsibility for their life and death.

The denial of help may represent the opposite. Some patients see denial as a sentence of death by torture, an edict that they must die without power, on their body's schedule, with all the suffering, discomfort, and indignity that may entail.

Questions to Ask Yourself

A patient's request for your help in dying can provoke various reactions. Because it often comes without warning, you may not feel adequately prepared for it. If you have never faced such a request, picture such a scenario now and imagine that you are asking yourself the following questions. Alternatively, if you have some experience with the situation, consider these questions in light of your past responses.

- Am I certain my patient has requested my help in dying? Did she specifically ask me? What did she actually say?

- What does the patient expect of me? Did she ask for any specific medication for this purpose?

- Does this appear to be an absolute decision, or did she say this was one of many options she was considering?
- Do I understand her motivation? Might the request serve some other purpose?
- Have I been honest with her about her prognosis?
- Have I been emotionally supportive?
- Did she say anything about wanting to change her current course of treatment?
- What was my initial reaction to her request? Was I shocked, angered, saddened? Did I reject her request, promise she wouldn't suffer, or give a noncommittal response?
- Do I feel obligated to help? If so, why?
- Do I see the request as a challenge to my skills, or do I feel pressure to attempt the impossible?
- Am I taking the request as a sign of personal failure or rejection?
- How might it affect my relationship with this patient in the future? Might I be less willing to work with her?

WHAT PATIENTS SAY ABOUT WANTING TO DIE

The final decision by a patient to approach you for aid in dying is rooted in a variety of concerns, some of which we have examined: intractable pain and intolerable suffering; diminished quality of life and loss of dignity; and erosion of autonomy. Though these are not the only motives patients may have for seeking your help, they are often the most crucial, and they are also the ones individuals are likely to feel most comfortable discussing.

Concerns About Physical Suffering

Obviously, the most important factor leading patients to consider an assisted death is their experience with the intolerable symptoms of an incurable or terminal condition. Although physical pain will usually loom large, the key issue is the overall physical experience of the illness. This may include fatigue, overwhelming weakness, fever, sleeplessness, dizziness, shortness of breath, severe nausea and vomiting, inability to eat or swallow, open wounds, stomach cramps, constipation, or diarrhea.

Also to be taken into account are the side effects of diagnostic procedures, treatment, and medications. Cancer patients, for example, regardless of any discomfort from the illness itself, frequently complain about the nausea, vomiting, loss of appetite and weight, and hair loss that result from traditional therapies. When such effects are added to the active symptoms of an illness, the combination can be intolerable and sometimes incapacitating. This is especially true when clinicians fail to communicate compassionately with patients or disregard their concerns. As one woman with a rare progressive neurological disorder told me:

It was bad enough feeling the onset of my symptoms, with the vertigo, the tingling, and the numbness. Had I been well and had energy, perhaps the tests and medications wouldn't have had the same effect. As it was, even a simple spinal tap sent me to the emergency room twice. The first time was for excruciating headaches; I needed a blood patch because of spinal fluid leakage. I had to go again, because the headaches didn't go away and I had severe vomiting and dizziness.

What made it worse was everyone telling me none of this was normal, with one neurologist saying I had no reason for being there, and another telling me that perhaps I also had meningitis. It took me nearly two weeks to get back on my feet.

A combination of physical symptoms can be seen clearly in the impact of AIDS and cancer, both of which can engender a multitude of physical complaints. AIDS, in particular, can affect nearly every organ in the body, including the eyes, brain, lungs, and digestive and nervous systems, as well as external and internal skin surfaces. It can result in massive weight loss, blindness, and dementia. Treatment is often specific to each condition and can vary from patient to patient. More conditions mean more medications, and this increases the potential for side effects and drug interactions.

Although many symptoms experienced during a life-threatening illness can be controlled, opportunities for patients to receive appropriate care are variable. Effective symptom control depends on clinicians who are skilled in listening and communicating, have training or experience in chronic pain management, are aware of the risks of undertreatment, appreciate the importance of carefully titrated dosages, and are willing to follow clinical practice guidelines. These qualifications are not always met.

In the SUPPORT study of 1995, more than 40 percent of hospitalized critical care patients had severe, potentially treatable pain for at least several days before they died. In an AIDS study by Breitbart and colleagues at Memorial Sloan-Kettering, only 15 percent of patients with HIV-related pain were found to have received adequate analgesia—and the results were even worse with respect to AIDS-related neuropathic pain. Although sensory neuropathy is experienced by about a third of all HIV patients and tricyclic antidepressants and anticonvulsants have been proved effective in controlling it, this study showed that only 6 percent of those with severe pain receive such medication. Clearly, pain control is being woefully underused in the treatment of our most severe diseases.

Concerns About Quality of Life

A patient's symptoms, and their effect on his energy and concentration, also limit his ability to engage in and enjoy many of the activities he previously took for granted. The impact on quality of life may begin with physical mobility, extend to sexual relations, and then spread to social life and work-related tasks. As the number of physical symptoms increases, even simple chores become difficult or impossible, and eventually the most basic activities of life—eating, sleeping, bathing, toileting, breathing without difficulty—are compromised.

Loss of these latter functions represents, for many patients, the final theft of dignity. The Remmelink study by van Delden and others on physician-assisted death in the Netherlands found that "loss of dignity" was the reason most often given for euthanasia requests. It was cited—alone or in connection with other factors—in 57 percent of the cases examined. By contrast, pain was cited as the only motive in 9.4 percent of cases.

Many prefer to use the more encompassing phrase *quality of life* to describe their reasons for considering assisted death. Several such individuals have told me that an exclusive focus on "pain" and "suffering" does little justice to the overall encounter with illness. The total impact of an illness, including the threat of death, must be taken into account, and an interrelated complex of physical, cognitive, and emotional factors acknowledged. Living in the throes of a life-threatening condition entails an all-consuming daily battle.

To many patients, "lack of quality of life" is the only way to describe the ongoing experience of illness and the massive personal loss it causes. In addition to the symptoms previously named, the challenges may include long, restless hours seeking less painful positions in which to sleep; frustrating attempts to find a balance between pain (or other symptoms) and the side effects of medications; constant clashes with clinicians over symptom relief; physical embarrassment when friends visit and loneliness when they do not; anguish at no longer being able to drive, to engage in former hobbies, to maintain sexual relations with one's spouse, to concentrate, to read . . . to fully live.

Concerns About Autonomy and Control

Some patients describe being motivated to die by the loss of their sense of autonomy that results from their physical condition. Some view the maintenance of an independent lifestyle as an absolute necessity, defining this as the ability to reside in one's own residence, to continue to engage in favorite pursuits, and to be self-sufficient with respect to one's own care. Others talk of maintaining physical mobility, of remaining alert, of never being completely bedridden, and of never needing to be cared for by others in one's home. And for more than a few patients, autonomy and independence mean never entering a long-term care facility or never submitting to final hospitalization or life-sustaining treatment.

Some patients use the terms *independence* and *autonomy* to describe their ultimate right to determine their destiny and to live and die on their own terms. These are boundaries they will never cross. For such individuals, taking control over death is often seen as an extension of maintaining control in life. To live and die autonomously is their sacred mandate and a matter of the highest honor. One nurse practitioner, talking about the assisted death of her elderly mother with early Alzheimer's, described this patient's concerns:

> Mom and I were out in the garden, behind her home where she'd lived for thirty years. And she began pulling out some of her favorite flowers, asking if they were weeds. She stopped, and then began crying, saying she didn't know the difference any more. A week later, she called me in a panic to ask for directions home from the store. This was the same store she'd driven to every day for years.
>
> Although eighty-seven, she'd been completely independent, but now couldn't drive or go out on her own. Her greatest fear was the onset of further confusion, because she knew she'd lose all independence and have to move out of her house. She didn't want to leave. That would've been too much for her. She wanted to die here. After talking about it for maybe three months, she then broke her hip, and it all came to a head, because she knew she'd have to move. I finally agreed to help.

Concerns of the Exhausted Patient

Often at the heart of the request for assisted death is a patient's emotional response to her overall experience—or "career"—as a patient. The request may be motivated by sheer exhaustion from the long road of illness and treatment that she has been forced to travel.

Whatever motives a patient has expressed to you for requesting help in dying—intolerable pain and suffering, a negative quality of life, the desire for control—her decision may also be driven by the constant battle she has waged against an illness for months or years.

This career includes major benchmarks such as diagnostic procedures, invasive surgeries, and therapies, as well as all the lesser events involved in an illness: office visits, blood workups, telephone calls for appointments, and all the discussions about the illness, treatment, and prognosis. As the illness slowly becomes a way of life, all of this can take a toll. For example, one man told me how even a simple office visit would affect his wife in the early stages of her career with cancer:

I'd come home from work and ask, "What'd you do today?" And she'd say, "I went to the doctor." That said it all. She'd worry about everything, and on these days it might take her hours to emotionally prepare. She couldn't get anything done. She couldn't eat or concentrate. She'd worry if her underwear was too frayed or sexy. She'd think about what she'd say, and how she'd say it, in the limited time she'd have with her doctor, and she'd worry how to get answers without being too demanding. Then she'd spend the rest of the day returning to normal. She'd be fine by the time I got home, but I knew what she'd gone through.

A career as a patient may affect every detail of life and have a significant impact on family members. As one woman told me, "For all of us, my illness has become a way of life. For me, it's a full-time job with no pay." Another woman shared excerpts from her journal:

My family is part of this. It involved them last night, as I prepared dinner, which I didn't eat. I had these tests this morning, so I fasted. They were concerned for me, and I felt awkward that my illness had once again intruded into their lives.

In dealing with patients and their requests for aid in dying, it is important to keep this career in mind. In many ways, you and other clinicians have become the patient's life. You add to her career with every office visit, test, and procedure. And when you are asked for help in dying, the request speaks of the cumulative emotional impact of this career. In the course of her illness, the patient has had to

- Prepare mentally and practically for an increasing number of exams, diagnostic procedures, and treatments, which has meant arranging time away from work, rescheduling or canceling activities, and in some cases, orchestrating transportation and child care

- Endure the physical and emotional discomfort, and the disruption of daily life, entailed in undergoing and recovering from exams, procedures, treatments, and medications, adjusting constantly to new dosages and drugs, and dealing with their side effects

- Await the results of tests with a mixture of anxiety and exhaustion, wondering if anything new will be learned, if it will affect her treatment, and if her clinician will answer her seemingly endless questions

- Ride the ever-shifting emotional currents of illness and treatment, responding with anxiety, optimism, or despair with every symptomatic change or comment from her clinician

- Face the eventual replacement of normal life with one based on illness, which will mean the redefinition of herself as an incurable or terminal patient

- Witness the emotional and practical impact of her illness, treatment, and potential death on significant others

Concerns About Future Conditions

In requesting aid in dying, not all patients feel comfortable talking about their fears of the future—fears of dementia, uncontrollable pain, loss of mobility, or other symptoms specific to their illness. They may be reluctant to discuss these concerns because they anticipate that you will not accept them as valid reasons for wanting to die. Their hesitation may also result from previous conversations in which clinicians have shied away from potentially negative topics. As one patient told me,

> Whenever I brought up the topic of what would happen down the line, my doctor kept saying, "Don't worry" and "Now's not the time to talk about that." This is probably the same thing he says to everyone. I honestly wanted to know what my cancer had in store for me. It made me feel like a child and just made me worry all the more.

Fear of future conditions is common among patients with life-changing diagnoses. Patients may worry about symptoms that have already plagued them to some extent, but they particularly worry about the onset of conditions and symptoms that are frequently linked to their specific diagnosis. Many illnesses, including certain cancers, progressive multiple sclerosis, Alzheimer's disease, and AIDS, have their predictable demons. AIDS, for example, is associated in the minds of patients with the prospect of blindness or dementia, and their fear is fed by easy access to medical information and by seeing the symptoms up close in their community of friends and fellow patients.

Although the conditions or symptoms that patients fear may never emerge, they still can be powerful motives for requesting an assisted death. I have talked with a number of patients about such concerns and have often heard them speak of the "inevitability" of dementia, blindness, the inability to swallow, or complete immobility. They may say that they have little interest in "waiting around for it."

Fear of increasing pain is also a common motive for considering an assisted death. For example, the wife of a man with metastasized prostate cancer once told me that her husband "could barely handle the pain" and "just knew it was only going to get worse." She explained that he hated every medication he had been given, didn't like the side effects, and "didn't want to wait too long before he got what he needed. He wanted to act before things got too bad."

Again, health professionals themselves are partially to blame for this fear, especially when they fail to appreciate the effect of a few misspoken words. For example, one woman told me how her mother had "panicked" as a result of a conversation she had had with her clinician. Suffering with a rare malignant tumor in her sinus cavity, she asked her clinician how she would know when she was "near the end." He replied, "Oh, you'll know. The pain will be absolutely excruciating." Earlier, she had refused a surgical procedure as it would have required removal of her left eye and adjacent bone. She saw this as "too much." After having a mastectomy five years prior, she "didn't want to have anything more cut out." Now distraught following her physician's comments, she and her daughter were calling everyone about obtaining a lethal drug to avoid that "excruciating" death.

Because of such fears, it is not unusual for patients to question every new symptom, seeing it as the beginning of an unacceptable end. However, rather than sharing their fears with their clinicians and describing their true motives for requesting help in dying, some patients mask them behind symptoms or conditions they feel are more acceptable or might carry more weight.

Concerns About Burdening Others

Another frequently hidden motive is the desire of patients to "not burden others" with their care. Several patients with whom I have talked, and numerous surviving family members I have interviewed, have explained the complexity of this motive. Patients claim that it arises partly from the desire to remain independent but also has its root in a strong concern for the practical needs of their spouses, partners, or other family members, who may be struggling to manage their own lives.

Some have described a fear that their prolonged care will physically and emotionally exhaust their spouses or family members. This fear can strike patients at any stage of an illness, whether they are actively undergoing treatment or needing full-time help because of their deteriorating physical condition. Certain cancer therapies, for example, involve almost daily treatments, often for weeklong periods staggered over several months. Unless patients are able to arrange alternative transportation, family members or friends will need to drive them to the hospital or cancer center, which can be problematic if these individuals work and cannot take off the necessary time. Moreover, not all patients live near these medical facilities. Any patient who has had to make heavy demands on his close circle simply to ensure that he gets to a treatment center may well balk later at having these same people provide around-the-clock care.

This level of practical help can be a particular problem when a primary caregiver is elderly or otherwise lacks the strength to take on the tasks of constant lifting, feeding, bathing, and toileting. But even when good family assistance is available, it is difficult to adequately care for a patient with a life-threatening illness, and home nursing may not be a financially feasible alternative. Residence in a long-term facility may be the only option.

Concerns About Financial Resources

Linked to the desire not to burden others with caregiving may be concerns of a more financial nature. Not everyone is insured or has adequate health coverage. Estimates suggest that the United States has roughly forty million uninsured, who lack coverage even by government health programs. In addition, experimental procedures or drugs that might save or prolong a patient's life often are not covered by major medical insurance plans or available through health maintenance organizations. The costs can be enormous. For example, experimental bone marrow transplants, which may offer a last, faint hope for certain cancer patients, can cost over $100,000. The expense of some of the most promising AIDS drugs, or of standard treatment and care for many other patients with life-threatening conditions, is often beyond the reach of those who are uninsured or underinsured.

For patients and families who do commit themselves to these enormous expenditures, the practical and emotional burdens can be heavy. There are patients who express the view that costly treatment, home nursing, or quality extended care is a "waste of money" under the circumstances. They view their funds as communal or family resources that could be better spent for the benefit of surviving family members. Some see their continued living as detrimental to the lives of others, both in the present and later. Nevertheless, it is no easy thing to have to choose between treatment and the retention of one's home or between full-time care and a university education for one's children or grandchildren.

Families usually do not make these decisions or actively voice these concerns. Instead, it is often patients who take responsibility for the economic bottom line. As a result, they may not divulge their knowledge of experimental procedures, dismissing them as "something that others can waste their money on." Or they may strike a bargain with family members to remain alive only as long as they find some quality in life, so that resources are not depleted "unnecessarily." When quality finally evaporates, they may make the decision to seek aid in dying.

Although economic concerns and the fear of burdening others seem to be questionable motives for deciding to die, this is not always the case. Certain patients appear to make such decisions selflessly, after thoughtfully weighing the financial impact of their continued treatment on their families. This can be seen in the following case with which I became familiar:

Alan was a fifty-year-old of middle income in the final stages of lung cancer. He had undergone surgery and therapies, but his cancer had widely metastasized with bone and liver involvement. Prior to his most recent hospitalization, he had been receiving home hospice care, with the majority of assistance provided by his wife and two young adult children.

He was now hospitalized for respiratory distress from pneumonia. In addition to labored breathing, he was suffering severe pain for which he was receiving morphine by use of a patient-controlled analgesia pump. He was also being provided oxygen. Despite his symptoms and palliative care, he was alert and communicative.

He had expressed his desire for assisted death on several occasions in recent weeks, both before and during this last hospitalization. Though he explained that he was suffering intolerably, his physician refused to help. Finally, he admitted that his most important motivation for requesting help was financial.

When Alan first got sick, he didn't leave his job but used accumulated vacation to cover his time off work. When this ran out, he began using his sick leave. Alan was especially concerned about "outliving" his sick leave. This would have meant going on disability, which would have resulted in a significant reduction in the survivor's pension his wife would receive after his death. He finally admitted to his physician and family that he wanted to die before the sick-leave benefits ran out. His family hesitantly agreed with his decision to die but said this was because of his intolerable suffering, not because of the financial considerations.

He was worried also about the large number of bills for his treatment that had not been covered by his medical plan. Although he and his wife owned a modest home, they had a mortgage, were helping one of their sons through college, and had limited savings. Alan's medical expenses would likely wipe out these savings. The risk of his dying even a week later was too difficult for Alan to accept. Nevertheless, his physician refused his request. With no other recourse, Alan refused further treatment and managed to die before his deadline.

Concerns About Isolation

There are some patients who, because of their feelings of social isolation, see themselves with few options and nowhere to turn. They may begin to actively explore the possibility of assisted death simply because they have no family, few friends, and limited financial resources. But regardless of the number of other people around, an incurable or terminal condition can be a lonely experience.

A person becomes especially isolated when she has no one to turn to for all the practical help, financial support, and caregiving that an illness requires. Under such circumstances, an incurable or terminal illness becomes an impossible challenge. Even early in the course of an illness, a patient may envision herself alone at home without care, or on the street, or warehoused with strangers in a convalescent facility. Patients have told me this is both a practical and an emotional issue for them. However, when discussing it as a motive for seeking aid in dying, they may emphasize the practical concerns. One man told me: "I'm not sad about being alone. It's the way I've lived my life. And I'm not about to change my ways now just because I'm dying."

The issue of isolation is particularly acute for those with incurable and degenerative conditions, who may be overwhelmed by being alone without support or financial resources. Such patients may anticipate these problems continuing for several years. One woman with multiple sclerosis told me:

> I have no family—no brothers or sisters, and my parents are dead. The man I loved, my partner for several years, died a few years back, and since then I've felt completely alone. I have a few friends, but it's not the same. And now I'm running out of money, can't live on Social Security, and can't ask my few friends for help. I know I could sell my car, which I'll have to do anyway, but it'd only give me enough money for another four months. My options aren't very good. I really don't see any reason continuing.

The lack of family and support mechanisms, combined with the physical and emotional effects of the illness, can prevent patients like this woman from taking the initiative to search for help from other sources, such as social workers, patient support organizations, and social service agencies.

There are also patients with living family members who nevertheless feel isolated and are led to explore the option of assisted death. They find it preferable to the alternative—making an overture for help to more distant relatives or to those from whom they are somewhat estranged.

Not all of us are close to our families of origin, our biological families. There can be significant emotional distance between family members or unfinished business that, according to some patients, "no one wants to complete." I have seen this frequently among gay male AIDS patients, who would rather turn to their friends for help. They may have left home years before and felt ostracized or cut off because of their sexual orientation. In other instances, families drift apart and have little in common. This is apparent in the following comments of a woman with ovarian cancer. Also apparent is her confusion about what she really wants.

> There's not much family left, and we're not close. My mother's elderly and my sister knows of my condition but, other than calling me a few times and sending a prayer card, hasn't offered to help. On the phone recently, she talked mostly about her three kids and didn't really ask me much.
>
> I have no desire to lose my independence, but it looks like I'll soon need round-the-clock care. Remaining at home isn't an option, and I wouldn't ask my sister if I could move in with her. Once, years ago, she told me that I'd better get my own life together, because she wouldn't be there for me. It might be different now, but I couldn't bring myself to ask.
>
> I wouldn't ask her to help out financially either. Once, after my husband left me, I had to ask for a loan. I paid it right back, but I never thought I'd hear the end of it. We've never really gotten along, and it would be pure hell to have to ask her for anything. I know a lot of it is me, but we just clash. None of this is a choice. So I'd rather remain independent as long as I can, then check out when the time comes.

DESPAIR

It is not uncommon during a patient's career with an incurable or terminal illness to descend into hopelessness, which may spur a request for help in dying. It is unusual, however, for patients to directly admit to you the depths of such despair, to define it as depression, or to speak of it in isolation from their physical concerns. Patients may hide this feeling because they fear you will not consider it adequate justification for assisting in suicide.

In psychotherapeutic settings, patients' fear of intervention by the therapist may make them even more reluctant to share their concerns. In both contexts, the only things they may be willing to admit are feelings of sadness or the impossible nature of their physical, social, and economic conditions.

Sometimes, however, the patient may not be entirely aware of the role that hopelessness plays as a motive for seeking your help. Though his sense of despair colors every interpretation of his circumstances, it resides beneath the surface, and he does not see it as the reason for his wanting to die. Other motives that he views as valid—pain, intolerable suffering, debilitating discomfort, diminished quality of life, or loss of dignity or independence—acquire much of their definition from this despair but are also distorted by it in ways that remain hidden to him.

Nevertheless, the more typical request does eloquently convey the fact that the patient no longer sees anything to live for:

- "My suffering is intolerable, I have no joy, or hope of having any, and I only know I can't go on like this."

- "I feel a total sense of loss, with my independence, dignity, quality gone, and no way to get back. It's useless to continue."

- "I just couldn't live . . . on a constant downhill slide. I can't even think about it. I feel so hopeless with that kind of life in front of me. . . . I've had more than my share of loss, and I don't want any more. I've lived a good full life. I feel at peace with my decision, but I prefer to die sooner rather than later."

Questions to Ask Yourself

The motives a patient expresses for seeking your help in dying can raise a number of issues for you, ranging from the quality of care you have provided to your feelings about assisted dying in general and this particular patient's decision to end her life. If a patient requests that you help her die, I recommend asking yourself the following questions:

- Am I satisfied that I fully understand my patient's concerns about pain, suffering, and the quality of her life?

- Have I provided her with ample opportunities to discuss her feelings about her illness, her fears about her prognosis, and her sense of despair?

- Have I given her opportunities to describe her dissatisfaction with the course of her treatment and with the measures I am taking to control her pain and discomfort?

- Have I explained the full range of side effects she might experience from each treatment? Have I expressed my willingness to do all I can to alleviate them?

- Is there anything I can do to provide my patient with greater control over her health care decisions?

- What can I do to reduce the daily impact of her illness? Can I do anything to alter her overall perception of her career as a patient?

- Is there anything I can do to ease the burden of care being borne by my patient and her family? Can I reduce the number of visits or procedures that are required of her?

- What information can I provide about social services, community support, and hospice care that might reduce her concerns about burdening others?

- How might I change the way I communicate with my patient so that her fears are more likely to be alleviated?

- Have I, in the most supportive way, detailed the likely future course of her illness, the level of discomfort she might experience, and my plans for responding to each change in her condition?

- Might financial concerns be underlying her request for my help? What is the likely economic impact of the treatments I have recommended, and what is the best projection of the total costs of her care?

- Do I consider my patient's physical and emotional motives for wanting to die valid? Might I ever consider them legitimate reasons for agreeing to help her die?

***

Patients seek aid in dying for any number of reasons, both physical and emotional, and there is not always one absolute reason. Nor does it mean that the final decision is unencumbered by emotional considerations. Instead, there are usually several factors that must come together, often over time. Ultimately, all components need to fit, and the patient's final reasons to die must outweigh the reasons to continue living. As a clinician, some of these factors may be under your control. For example, pain and physical suffering can often be alleviated. Similarly, fear of future intolerable conditions can be allayed by providing factual information, communicating compassionately, demonstrating a willingness to stand by and work with the patient as long as necessary, and agreeing to cooperate with hospice staff during the final stages of care. However, prior to taking these responsive actions, you need to obtain a deep understanding of the patient's motives, both expressed and unexpressed.

Whatever those motives are, the request for assisted dying can be interpreted in two distinct ways. Seen through one lens, it represents a desire to end the patient's relationship with you, which may have begun years before. You may therefore view it as evidence of professional failure. But beyond that, the request asks you to let go of curing and caring, the essence of your vocation. You may ask yourself, "Should I abandon healing and violate the laws and norms of my profession?" "Should I accept failure and grant my patient ultimate power over his own death?" "Should I end this relationship by ending my patient's life?"

Seen through another lens, however, the request symbolizes not an end but a desire to change the nature of your relationship. In this view, diagnosis, treatment, and healing are not left behind but incorporated into a broader form of care that accepts death and rejects suffering—a form of care based on compassion and intuition. You might welcome this shift as a way to close the gap between yourself and your patient and to move from treating disease and symptoms to treating the patient's very soul.

For these reasons, a patient's request for your help, whether he knows it or not, is more than a simple plea for a lethal prescription. It is a call for honesty, trust, mutual respect, and the deepest level of professional concern. It is an invitation for you to participate fully—clinically and emotionally—in what may be the most critical period of the patient's life. However, in these circumstances, aid in dying is neither easily provided nor instantly denied.

Your willingness to at least consider this plea for help can do much to address the patient's physical and emotional concerns. At this juncture, you may be able to perform your best work—listening to the person's innermost thoughts, looking deeply at his reasons for wanting to die, responding humanely with both clinical skills and compassion, all the while accepting the inevitability of his death. You are called on to set aside your traditional role and to become a different type of healer, a fusion of clinician and midwife who can provide the patient with a safe and easy passage out of this life.

In the following chapter, we will look at the request for assisted death at this deeper level. I will provide some tools for assessing and responding to requests and for gaining a better understanding of the motives and concerns we have just examined.

3

Responding to Requests for Help

A patient's request for assisted dying represents one of the greatest challenges you will face as a clinician and can take you to the very depths of what it means to be a helping professional. It can be the touchstone you use to test your ethical beliefs, weigh the limits of mercy, and define the boundaries of your professional behavior. Depending on your viewpoint, it may hold out the promise of participation in a person's most momentous transition or threaten your professional identity and the central meaning of your skills as a clinician.

When confronted with a request, you have four options: evading it, refusing the request outright, agreeing to help, and holding off a decision until you have fully explored the patient's underlying motives and innermost concerns. I find the use of evasive tactics and false promises reprehensible in their dishonesty and paternalism. I also believe there is too much to be gained from open dialogue to prematurely shorten the process by either immediately denying or agreeing to a request.

I therefore recommend a deeper exploration of the reasons behind such a demand. This can enable you to identify underlying motives and previously unknown symptomatic problems and to provide opportunities to discuss all options without the risk of closing down communication.

However, talking with a patient about assisted dying will demand your best skills in communication. It requires that you listen to her with an open heart and mind, and that you leave behind any ego investment you may have in her treatment. This presupposes a willingness on your part to accept change in the nature of the relationship you have had with this patient, and carries the expectation that you set aside your more traditional role to embark on a new path, one you may be hesitant to walk on.

CONSIDERING HOW TO RESPOND

Like many clinicians, you may not want the responsibility entailed in such a dialogue. You may find it easier to focus on the clinical aspects of helping and healing and to concentrate on the physical needs of the patient. But as you know from experience, the treatment of incurable and potentially terminal illnesses calls for a much more holistic approach. The fight against the all-encompassing physical devastation of such illnesses as cancer and AIDS certainly requires your very best clinical skills, but it also demands an openness on your part to listen to the patient's concerns, to separate physical from emotional complaints, and to consider the patient's fear and uncertainty as seriously as you might attend to her more visible needs.

The Temptation of Avoidance

Clinicians are not always inclined to engage in such efforts. There are those who, in their desire to avoid talking about assisted death or a patient's ultimate fears, retreat from open communication. In response to a patient's request for help, you may be tempted to say, "You don't see me giving up here, do you?" or "I don't want to hear any more talk about death," or "I've seen people far worse off than you who've made complete recoveries," or "There's a lot more we can do that we haven't yet tried." Although you may believe such sentiments, and they may be partly true, such words can seem patronizing to patients who are looking for an open and compassionate response.

Going the extra mile, however, is not always easy. Some clinicians feel that agreeing to enter into dialogue on such issues opens a Pandora's box. Like them, you may prefer the path of avoidance for various reasons:

- Given your time constraints, a heavy patient workload, and complex issues of reimbursement, especially in a managed care environment, you may want to limit your focus to the patient's here-and-now health concerns.

- You may feel that you lack the communication and therapeutic skills needed to discuss such issues and to deal effectively with the terror patients can experience in the face of death.

- You may believe that discussion of death detracts from the positive emphasis on healing that a patient needs to maintain.

- You may shy away from such discussion because of your own personal anxieties about death, or because you fear the implication of professional failure.

- You may be concerned about the risks of discovery, loss of license, or criminal prosecution.

- You may anticipate that you will be emotionally overwhelmed by a request or somehow lack the strength to resist it.

Beneath your preference for avoidance may be deeper issues. You may view the request as a personal rejection by a patient, a rebuff for the failure of treatment, a symbol of this person's lack of faith in your skills as a health professional, and a rejection of everything you have come to believe about the power of medicine to heal, to provide comfort, and to dispense daily miracles. As one physician told me:

I've never forgotten the first patient who asked. I had an immediate visceral response: "How dare this person do this!" I was put on the defensive, that I wasn't doing enough, though I was. I felt angry. On the spot. I didn't know how to respond, but I didn't say no at the time. Later, I saw this had been all about me and decided not to take it personally, but to ask how I could better serve the patient.

The Risks of Refusing

An outright refusal to help a patient die carries its own risks. Importantly, it can affect the quality of your future communication by creating a sense of discomfort between the two of you. Because the patient may be ashamed of having asked, or embarrassed, or angry, or disappointed at having been rebuffed, he may find it difficult to participate in a relaxed flow of communication. This increases the risk that he will sink into a sense of isolation and abandonment and build a defensive wall that effectively excludes discussion of other concerns. Moreover, refusing a patient's request does not necessarily prevent an assisted death or suicide. Instead, it may turn the patient toward family and secrecy in a quest for other sources of lethal medications or means to end his life.

The wall may have two builders. Denying a request can make the clinician uncomfortable about seeing the patient again. Unless a request is managed with compassion and a promise that one will do one's best, the possibility exists that it will be repeated, with further disappointment for the patient and additional uneasiness for the health professional.

Although it is not ethical to do so, some physicians or nurses might seek to avoid such a patient. One physician I interviewed said that, in more than one instance, enough was enough: "I told them if this was what they wanted, they could just go elsewhere." By contrast, another clinician told me:

I avoid taking a position on this issue, or I wind up abandoning patients who are convinced they want to do it. If you tell them you're against it, they want to give up on you. The worst

decision is for a doc to walk away, instead of being there helping through to the end, whatever it takes.

The Temptation to Help Quickly

One might imagine that hardly any clinician would immediately
agree to help, but many do. For example, in a survey of AIDS practitioners in the San Francisco Bay Area by Lee Slome and colleagues, fully 48 percent said they were "likely" or "very likely" to
prescribe a lethal dose of medication, on first request, to a hypo-
thetical patient with severe wasting syndrome, painful oral ulcers,
and a mildly depressed mood who had responded poorly to treatment for his third episode of *Pneumocystis carinii* pneumonia. In the
event that the patient was "adamant about getting assistance," 51
percent would do so. (In this survey sample, 53 percent admitted to
having assisted in the death of at least one patient.)

Although a rapid response may provide the patient with a certain kind of security, it can close the door on deeper communication. Further, it can send the patient the wrong message by reducing
him to a biological entity and disregarding the complexity of his
problems, some of which may not be physical and perhaps could be
resolved by other means. Instant agreement may thus short-circuit
a patient's search for other ways to combat suffering. It also ignores
any other objectives the patient may have in making the request,
such as finding a purpose in continued living, receiving personal
validation, and obtaining assurance that the clinician will be there
until the end. As a hospital ethics committee chairperson told me:

> I'm horrified at physicians who give lethal prescriptions the
> first time they're asked. I think that's a grave disservice to the
> humanity of the person you're face to face with.

Another physician, an oncologist, said he felt that some of his
colleagues might see a request "as a chance to relinquish responsibility and a sense of failure" by handing over the reins of life and

death to the patient. A hospice nurse I interviewed described immediate agreement as a "byproduct of autonomy and not knowing where patients' rights end." Although she agreed that "assistance should be available in some cases," she felt it was "an abdication of one's duty as a health professional to provide [aid in dying] willy-nilly."

A particularly interesting viewpoint was outlined to me by a hospice medical director in Northern California, who saw agreement as a way of reestablishing control in the midst of uncertainty:

> We're addicted to curing our patients, to success, and some of us have a dismal time accepting patients dying. In my opinion, many doctors give their patients lethal doses because it's the one way they can stay in control in the face of death. God forbid that they should let go and let the disease take its course, and then walk with the patient through that. That's very difficult to do compared to staying in control and letting the patient stay in control and giving them a lethal dose of medication.

THE INITIAL EXPLORATION OF A REQUEST

Regardless of your position on the issue of assisted dying, it should be obvious by now that there is much to be gained by openness in talking about it. I strongly encourage you to take this leap and delve into the topic as deeply as you can, conducting what might be termed a preliminary exploration. Such a journey can be especially fruitful in identifying and addressing the full range of a patient's needs. It calls for a willingness to ask searching questions, to listen deeply, and to show genuine concern for the person's journey and ultimate fate so that you come to understand her on her own ground. You need not be a therapist to embark on this task, but you do need to be open to encountering the patient's human heart.

This initial exploration is triggered by the request. You would do well to reflect carefully on its wording and any explanation the patient has offered as to motives. This may provide you with much of the information you need to proceed further—to frame the questions that will lead to a better understanding of the patient's concerns. You might consider the following issues:

- Why is this patient asking for my help?
- Why is she asking now?
- Is she keeping all options open or making immediate plans to die?
- Is this an understandable desire on her part?
- Is it supported by her physical condition and quality of life?
- Do the reasons given suggest another way I can respond and better serve her needs?

The most important questions for you to consider are "Why?" "Why now?" and "When?" The first type of question provides you with the patient's justification for both wanting to die and asking for your help. The others allow you to relate a patient's expressed motives to what you already know of her current physical status, quality of life, prognosis, possible future conditions, and other factors. Answers to these questions can also caution you about the seriousness of the patient's desire to die, the immediacy with which she plans to act, and possible impulsiveness in her decision.

The ease of finding such answers varies. For example, in one case, the fact that an end-stage cancer patient's symptoms have steadily become intolerable and difficult to manage makes a request, on the surface, more reasonable. Such facts can focus your attention immediately on a set of issues, ranging from specific symptoms to emotional concerns, and can help you determine the direction of your response and the types of questions you need to ask.

In another case, however, the knowledge that a patient's condition has been unchanged and quite manageable for some time can make your preliminary exploration more difficult, yet also more imperative. The patient's unchanged physical condition should alert you to look elsewhere for motives—to new factors, changes in the patient's life, or any number of psychosocial elements of which you have previously been unaware. You may find the task daunting. The answer may be as subtle as a hidden state of hopelessness or depression, or it may be as obvious as a patient's long-held personal philosophy about autonomy in end-of-life choices and her desire to finally prepare for the inevitability of death in the face of a terminal illness.

Whether he knows it or not, a patient who requests your help in dying is opening the door to dialogue. A request demands a response, and this should be more than a lethal prescription. The most important response you can make is to do all you can to completely understand the person under your care. Merely grasping a patient's expressed motives is not good enough.

To make even an initial assessment of the situation, you would do well to learn as much as possible about this person who has asked you to help him die. You need to consider what health-related and non-health-related factors might be influencing his decision. In this regard, you need to uncover any changes that have taken place in his home environment, economic situation, or caregiving arrangements. The patient's entire psychosocial life is grist for the mill. As a physician friend once told me:

> To me, assisted suicide is one of the most intimate acts I can imagine. If I were thinking about helping a patient to die, I would certainly need to know how he lived, the kind of life he had, his likes and dislikes. I'd probably have to know him well, meet his family, have dinner with him, know the designs on his dinnerware. And even then this might not be enough.

Without going this far, there are some questions you might begin asking to develop a stable base for your ongoing exploration. Later, there are other questions you can ask that relate more specifically to the motives this person has expressed for wanting your help. The information that you thus accumulate can be used to elicit more hidden motives and to assess such issues as the patient's competence in making the request and whether it was made voluntarily. The information can also help you uncover depression or other emotional factors that you must consider before any decision on assistance is made.

But we need to begin at the beginning, and this requires that you ask the very simplest of questions. I list here some of the most basic, by general category:

- *Impulsivity:* "How long have you been thinking about this?"

- *Certainty:* "Are you absolutely certain about this decision? How long have you been absolutely certain? Do you have any doubts?"

- *Immediacy:* "Are you planning on doing this any time soon? Have you made up your mind completely?"

- *Physical condition:* "Have there been any recent changes in your physical condition or quality of life that you haven't yet told me about? Is there anything I can do in terms of other treatment, or a referral to a specialist, that might help you now?"

- *Other motives:* "Is there one overriding reason for your decision? Are there any reasons other than what you've just told me? Is there anything else going on with you that I should know about? Have there been any changes at home that have been affecting you?"

- *Caregiving:* "How is the quality of your care at home? Are you satisfied? Have there been any changes there of which I should be aware?"

- *Philosophy:* "Is this something you believe in strongly? How long have you believed this?"

- *Secrecy:* "Does your family (spouse, partner, parents, siblings, children) know what you want to do? If not, why haven't you told them? Does anyone else (friend, minister, therapist) know what you want to do?"

- *Family dialogue:* "Does your family know how you feel about your situation? If not, why not? Have you had a chance to really talk with them about it?"

- *Effects on family:* "If your family knows about your decision, do they support it? Are they opposed in any way? Do they agree that now is the right time for you to do this, or would they prefer that you wait? Have you considered how this might affect them?"

- *Counseling:* "Have you talked about this with a counselor, minister, spiritual adviser, or other health professional? Without disclosing anything you or this person consider to be confidential, can you tell me what he or she said? How did that make you feel? Would you be willing to talk to someone else about what's going on?"

- *Plans:* "Have you made any specific plans? Is anyone aware of them? What is it that you are hoping I will do?"

- *Alternatives:* "Have you considered any alternatives? Would you be willing to let me work with you on these problems? Are you open to talking with someone about the advantages of hospice? Could I meet with you and a significant other to discuss all the options?"

These types of questions cover a range of initial concerns you may have, but they do not cover all the issues. For example, they do not touch on the specific expressed motives of the patient or on the possibilities of despair, depression, and other psychosocial influences.

It is unlikely that even your most in-depth dialogue would include every question I have listed. On the other hand, many other questions will probably arise, triggered by the initial answers you receive. The course of inquiry you choose will obviously vary from patient to patient. Your questions will depend, for example, on the request itself, the person's condition, and her declared motives.

RESPONDING TO THE COMPLEXITY OF MOTIVES

There is seldom a single reason why a patient seeks help in dying. Usually, there is a combination of physical, social, and emotional forces. Some of these elements are explicitly expressed in the request itself or are made explicit through the exploratory questions you ask. Others are unexpressed and become apparent only with further probing.

A patient may willingly describe a number of motivating factors, such as physical suffering, quality of life, and the desire for independence and control. In-depth discussion may subsequently elicit additional factors such as fear of future symptoms, anxiety about the burden of care (or the lack of caregiving), financial concerns, fear of abandonment, and despair about ever seeing an improvement in health. It should be noted also that intractable pain and symptomatic suffering are rarely experienced in isolation from other physical concerns, such as the loss of skills and diminished desire to engage in previously enjoyed activities.

Figure 3.1 is suggestive of some of these interconnections. Although it is not based on empirical research, it does reflect many of the linkages I have witnessed in group sessions and in hundreds of conversations I have had with those suffering from terminal or life-altering conditions. You might use it as a rough model for thinking about the specific motives that may be influencing your patient. Of course, these interrelationships of motives, expressed or not, can vary from case to case, and you may find many unique elements.

This diagram indicates that physical pain and suffering combined with diminished abilities can create a chain of effects, beginning with erosion of the patient's sense of independence and control, dignity, and overall quality of life. No longer can this person actively engage with the physical world, participate in social life, or even define himself as a creative or sexual being. If young,

FIGURE 3.1 Interrelationships of Motivations.

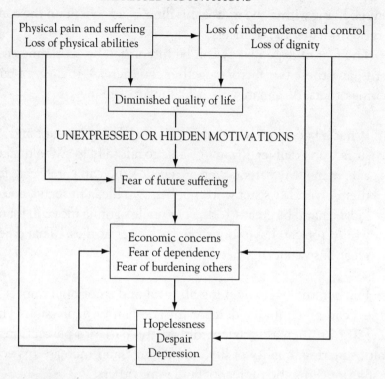

EXPRESSED MOTIVATIONS

Physical pain and suffering
Loss of physical abilities

Loss of independence and control
Loss of dignity

Diminished quality of life

UNEXPRESSED OR HIDDEN MOTIVATIONS

Fear of future suffering

Economic concerns
Fear of dependency
Fear of burdening others

Hopelessness
Despair
Depression

the patient has to relinquish thoughts of marriage, partnership, pro-creation, or active parenthood. It seems that a permanent line now separates this person from those who can still maintain the hope of love, partnership, travel, a career, and a future.

This diminishment can provoke an increased fear of further physical changes and dependency, leading in turn to a general sense of hopelessness. "What next?" a patient may ask. "What more can I expect, and when?" This person may validly feel that his life will never be as it once was, that it effectively is over before it has reached its true completion, that he will never be able, like those around him, to plan and realize a life path but instead will be dependent on others for the simplest acts, even perhaps for the fulfillment of his basic human needs. This once creative, self-made, independent being, a person who shaped his own world, now finds himself living within the walls of his illness, dependent on the comfort of intimates and strangers.

The fear of dependency can be intensified by economic concerns, and these two factors together can increase the fear of burdening others. As a man with AIDS once asked me:

> What'll I do when the money runs out? The restaurant and store won't deliver, I won't be able to afford help. Who'll take care of me? My parents who are aged? Who can barely care for themselves? My sister who's got her own life, a husband, and kids? That'd be great. "Kids, your uncle's gonna move in for a while. You can have your room back after he dies." That'd be great. Just what they need.

Further, the overwhelming physical and emotional impact of illness can precipitate a descent into despair or depression. This may in turn increase anxiety, distort the patient's perception of pain, suffering, quality of life, and dignity, and increase his economic concerns and his fear of burdening others.

UNCOVERING THE MOTIVES BEHIND THE PATIENT'S CONCERNS

In the previous chapter, we looked at a number of reasons patients may give to justify their request for your aid in dying. In this section, we will look beneath the surface of those expressed motives for deeper, underlying concerns. We will also consider possible responses to them.

If you are a physician or nursing professional and are considering the possibility of assisting in a patient's death, you are like a jury member who needs to be convinced beyond a reasonable doubt.

How do you proceed? More than anything, you need to listen with a mixture of heart and healthy skepticism. I strongly encourage you to use all the resources and information you can gather. Eventually, if you decide to proceed further, you would do well to utilize the resources of a trusted mental health professional. But for now, your task is simply to communicate, to ask questions, and to obtain answers, while continuing to provide your compassionate support and professional expertise.

Be aware, however, that you may not be successful in this effort. You may not discover clues to what is hidden, or anything other than what the patient has already told you. There are those who will resist your every effort to probe deeper. A patient may block you by refusing to answer even seemingly simple questions, by leading you down blind alleys, or by making you feel intrusive. You may be used to such communication difficulties. If you are not, it is important to stand your ground and make no decision that in any way causes you discomfort.

Physical Suffering

There is a large body of research that defines the concept of suffering in patients with advanced terminal illnesses. Kathleen Foley, chief of the pain service at Memorial Sloan-Kettering Cancer Center, identified three major elements of suffering in her 1997 editorial in the *New England Journal of Medicine*: "pain and physical symptoms," "psychological distress," and "existential distress."

As we have seen, pain and other uncontrolled symptoms can interfere with a patient's quality of life, sleep patterns, and previously normal physical activities, including his social interactions. They can also affect his sense of independence and control. Further, lack of success in treating such conditions can give rise to increased fear of future conditions, wariness about additional treatment, and general emotional exhaustion.

The patient may feel increasingly out of control and may lose his openness to physical and emotional support from others. As a result, he feels both angry that "nothing works" and guilty for taking it out on those closest to him. Feeling trapped in his suffering, he also may begin to see himself as a burden on others. This increases psychological distress and feelings of futility, hopelessness, and meaninglessness. He may keenly desire to escape from further suffering, further treatment, and further burdening of others. He might say:

> I'm tired of suffering like this. I've had more than my share, and nothing has worked. I've put up with it long enough, feel it's hopeless to continue, and I really don't want to go on like this any longer, just waiting for everything to get worse.

Exhaustion and hopelessness are the primary themes in this statement. The patient is "tired," but is he tired only of pain? And does he feel "hopeless" only because his physical condition is hopeless?

Confronted with such a statement, your task is to find its meaning. You may find a partial answer by indicating your willingness to do all you can to alleviate the patient's pain by means of aggressive symptom management (which I will describe in Chapter Five). Or you might suggest referring the patient to hospice or a doctor who is experienced in palliative care. If the patient rebuffs such overtures, physical suffering may not be his only motive. It will then be critical to determine what else he may feel tired and hopeless about. Beneath the statement, the patient may also be saying:

- "I'm tired of not being able to live like other people."
- "I'm tired of others not listening to how miserable I feel, of discounting my suffering, and not being willing to talk to me about my dying."
- "I'm tired of others telling me I'm going to get well and implying it's somehow my fault that I'm getting worse."
- "I'm tired of all the disappointments and losses."

The patient may be asking for others, including you, to listen and validate his feelings. Your best response might be to give him permission to talk about his exhaustion, by saying, "I know you're suffering—it must not be easy" or "You must have a lot of things, besides pain, that exhaust you."

You might then follow up by asking:

- "Does anyone else know how bad you feel?"
- "Do you feel you can talk about this with anyone? Is anyone supportive emotionally?"
- "You said that you expect everything to get worse. What do you fear the most?"

The answers to such questions can help you in designing a course of action and in negotiating with the patient what is and is not acceptable in terms of future treatment and overall medical care. For example, he may be most fearful of facing intolerable pain, or being hospitalized at the end of his life, or being subjected to invasive procedures. Only after you are aware of his specific concerns can you act to allay his fear and engage him in planning a course of action.

Independence and Control

As I showed in Chapter Two, some patients readily speak of independence and control as either primary or additional motives in asking for your help. These concepts may well be drawn from a patient's philosophical beliefs. They may also reflect ways in which she defines herself in relation to the world: standing apart, not needing anyone, not answering to anyone, not burdening anyone, or not changing her behavior for anyone.

However, hidden within such a motive may well be its flip side: fear of dependency and loss of control, and even deep feelings of loneliness and social isolation, of vulnerability and helplessness. Therefore, when a patient says, "I want to remain independent," be aware that she already may feel "out of control," that her illness has robbed her of control in the workplace and at home, as well as control of her body, her sexuality, her energy, and the resources that might meet her needs. Thus the request for an assisted death may also be a desire to:

• Escape current or perceived future loss of control
• Maintain whatever degree of control exists in the present
• Gain control over what the patient perceives as being least controllable—life itself and its end

Similarly, an emphasis on independence may be rooted in a fear that there is no one who cares and can be depended on, that one will be abandoned, hurt emotionally, or left alone at the end. This can be seen in the following example drawn from my own experience.

At the request of a friend, I met with a woman who told me that she was thinking about assisted suicide as a way out of metastasized breast cancer. She explained that she believed adamantly in "independence" and wanted to remain in control.

I proceeded by asking, "You're married. What does your husband think about this?" She responded by saying that her husband had managed her life, told her what she felt, what she did not feel, and what she should feel. She further admitted that she had not shared her thoughts with him about an assisted death, because he seldom listened or acknowledged what she had to say. She explained that having a prescription would give her the ultimate control over her death—control that her husband would not know about.

Upon further probing, she finally admitted, "I really don't think he's ever going to be there for me, emotionally." She added, "I can't imagine being bedridden and trapped alone, not being able to talk about it."

This case shows how the presence of other, unresolved, factors can underlie apparently straightforward motives. With this in mind, you might pose questions to elicit a response about the fear of losing control, or of dependency, or the person's need for emotional support. For example,

- "If you don't end your life, is there anyone to help care for you?"
- "Do you have anyone you can depend on?"
- "Is there anything else that might give you a sense of control?"
- "Is there anything I can do to make you feel more in control?"
- "Do you have a counselor with whom you can talk about your concerns?"

In our culture, men have particular difficulty with issues of control and independence. Overall, they do not do as well as women in effectively dealing with illness, in expressing their emotions, or in facing grief and loss. Moreover, they do not always recognize their need for help or know how to ask for it. They may not feel comfortable discussing their concerns even with their clinicians. Hospice professionals, especially hospice social workers and counselors, can be especially helpful in such cases, being particularly adept at sensitive communication with patients and skilled in bringing families into the dialogue.

The Burden of Care

As we have seen, worry about burdening others may be tied to fear of dependency, economic concerns, and a perceived loss of dignity.

Patients may feel that the needs of others are more important than their own, and that imposing on them cannot be justified. Some take it upon themselves to be arbiters of the best interests of the people close to them, even when those individuals might openly welcome the opportunity to help.

Like other motives, a patient's desire not to burden others with the physical or financial demands of her care may mask several feelings. This can be seen in another example:

In a discussion group I facilitated, a man said that he had no desire to burden his married daughter with his care. He explained that she was now finally settled with a young child and had just entered college, after having had a difficult adolescence. His daughter and her husband were struggling but doing well and needed "no further stress."

In response, I asked, "Do you think you can reduce your daughter's stress by dying without warning, before she's had time to really accept your illness?" He replied, "If she knew my plans, it would only cause her more stress. She shouldn't have to be burdened with anything." I then asked, "Are you sure there's nothing the two of you still need to work out?" This question proved to be a watershed.

Gradually, he admitted that he had never resolved his long-standing guilt over walking out of his marriage two decades before, effectively abandoning his daughter for several years, beginning when she was four.

Using this as a lever, I asked, "Do you think she might see your suicide as a second abandonment? Have you thought about giving her a chance to work out the first, and then letting her decide about the rest?"

These questions, although intrusive, prevented this man from making an ill-advised choice. Believing that he was acting out of love, he ran the risk of leaving a very different type of legacy. This example shows the power of questions and the benefits that can come from taking a tough stand to get at the truth.

The desire not to burden others may also be motivated by low self-esteem. This can be a sign of depression or a natural effect of a life-altering illness. In our culture, self-esteem is more easily maintained by those who are healthy. Those with terminal or life-altering illnesses tend to be removed from the most common sources of self-worth, which include career, financial achievements, social role, community service, appearance, and sexuality, to say nothing of health and fitness. Obviously, this notion of burdening others varies according to the strength of family ties, personal and family values, culture, and religious beliefs.

For many individuals, however, economics plays a crucial role. As the financial underpinnings of self-image disappear, patients who have identified their own value with their monetary resources may begin to see themselves without worth—in more than one sense.

As this and other sources of self-esteem diminish, the patient's sense of her value within the family and among friends can be seriously damaged. This in turn can alter her view of how her care might impact those around her. She may come to believe that she is "in the way" or "a burden to others"—unless she can somehow give as much as she receives. As the patient's estimate of her own importance declines, her view of the importance of others' needs may be unrealistically overemphasized.

At the extreme, such a person may fear that she is not wanted. In some cases, it is easier for a patient to actively pursue death than to discuss the issue with her family or wait to find out whether her fears are warranted. This reflects the problems that many individuals have in communicating any of their concerns within a relationship. It may also reflect strained interpersonal relationships and the perception that support is not to be had. The range of these underlying feelings, any of which may serve as unexpressed motives, can be seen in Table 3.1.

ASSESSING RATIONALITY AND UNCOVERING DEPRESSION

Nearly all of us spend our time participating in the social world, focusing on meeting the daily needs of a life that we expect has a future. We believe there will be a tomorrow, and a day after. We expect that there will be time to attain our personal goals and to establish new objectives and tasks as we go forward. We anticipate that we will have time for a career, recreational endeavors, visits to old friends, and opportunities to pay back our social, familial, and financial debts. And we may expect that we will be able to resolve any regrets and incompleteness in our social relationships. When

TABLE 3.1 Expressed and Unexpressed Motives.

Expressed Motive	"It's better like this. My husband has a lot of his own worries, my kids have their own lives. I no longer see any purpose in staying around. I'm no longer useful, and I don't want to burden others with my care."
Unexpressed Motives	"I'm afraid of putting people out." "I'm afraid I'll be seen as a burden." "I'm afraid I already am a burden." "I've burdened them enough in life." "I'm afraid others don't love me enough."

we think of death, we often do so distantly, imagining that it will come only after we have met our objectives. To think that it will descend on us before then can be unbearable. But this conception of the unbearable is exactly what is thrust on the patient with a terminal or life-altering condition.

Such an illness is a form of limbo. It presents a patient with the dilemma of living while possibly dying. In fact, in this transitional phase, the patient experiences both living and dying simultaneously, and she fights to hold onto life while she gradually loses hold of many of its components. As her physical abilities and previously vital aspects of personhood fade, she observes death in preview.

At the mind's edge, where a clear portrait of the future could previously be seen, such a patient may now glimpse only the darkness of death, disappointment, and fear. That darkness may be filled with the emotional debris she has never fully faced. And her current plight adds its own debris. There are feelings she both wants and does not want to confront or wants to share but tells herself— or is told by others—she must keep hidden. As one clinician commented to me, "The cliff that people fall off is actually there; it's a desperate time."

During this phase, it is not unusual for a patient either to look away from the edge and deny its existence or to be drawn closer toward it. But there are those who may seek death itself to avoid this encounter, as well as those who may seek it later during the experience. Immersed in darkness and despair, they are convinced that there is no other way out.

Uncovering Hopelessness and Depression

It is my belief that a request for aid in dying, under certain circumstances, can be a rational and reasonable response to an incurable or terminal condition. Many patients near the end of their lives do suffer intolerably, experience great changes in the quality of their existence, and arrive at a juncture where the continuation of living is an unbearable burden, both physically and emotionally. For some, the ordeal of suffering is a motivation in itself. For others, the overall quality of life may be impacted to such a degree that a conscious decision to die is seen by them as a rational solution.

The fact that patients are "hopelessly" ill does not, of course, mean that they are necessarily more rational about death than the general population or that their decision to die is always well reasoned. Some, for example, are at far higher risk and have an increased pathological impulse for suicide than others. Nevertheless, I do believe that such patients, on the average, do have more valid reasons than the rest of us for wanting to end their lives.

Staunch opponents argue otherwise, claiming that *rational suicide* is an oxymoron, that no rational person would ever truly contemplate or complete such an act. According to this view, suicide by a person in perfect physical health and a request for aid in dying by someone who is incurably or terminally ill are equivalent. Regardless of the motivation, such an act or request is seen to result from one or more psychiatric disorders. Studies are often cited that link suicide to depression or alcoholism or find a high incidence of depression in cancer and AIDS patients. The suggestion is that depression by itself is the cause of the request. If an individual is depressed, runs the argument, his cognitive functioning is also impaired, so that rational decisions about life and death are impossible. As Kathleen Foley has stated in testimony before Congress:

> Given the complexities of the medical and psychological states of patients with advanced disease and the dearth of trained health care professionals with expertise in the care of the dying, it is hard to believe that suicide is ever really rational.

I prefer Edwin Shneidman's statement in *Suicide as Psychache* that "suicide is not a psychiatric disorder." Shneidman points out that "all persons who commit suicide—100 percent of them—are perturbed, but they are not necessarily clinically depressed (or schizophrenic or alcoholic or addicted or psychiatrically ill)." I would add that many who are terminally and incurably ill are more than simply "perturbed"; they are experiencing intolerable physical suffering.

Nevertheless, the decision to die can also be motivated by what Richard Heckler has termed a "penetrating hopelessness"—a loss of faith that can lead to suicide. At times, tunnel vision can set in, rooted in hopelessness and a restricted view of options. In this patient's narrow view, it may seem completely natural and reasonable to want to die.

One of your tasks as a clinician is to look for visible signs of depression and to make an attempt to uncover evidence of its hidden presence. The obvious place to begin is with an understanding of the official definition of depression in the current bible of mental illness, the American Psychiatric Association's *Diagnostic and Statistical Manual of Mental Disorders*, fourth edition (DSM-IV), which describes several observable features of a major depressive episode. According to DSM-IV, these features include

> a period of at least 2 weeks during which there is either depressed mood or the loss of interest or pleasure in nearly all activities. . . . The individual must also experience at least four

additional symptoms drawn from a list that includes changes
in appetite or weight, sleep, and psychomotor activity; decreased energy; feelings of worthlessness or guilt; difficulty
thinking, concentrating, or making decisions; or recurrent
thoughts about death or suicidal ideation, plans, or attempts.

In addition, these symptoms should cause "clinically significant distress or impairment in social, occupational, or other important areas
of functioning."

As you will immediately see, the presence of depression in an
incurable or terminal patient may not be easy to diagnose, as many
of its observable features are typical of such patients. Several of the
listed symptoms are also common side effects of treatment. These
include impairment in social or occupational functioning, changes
in appetite or weight or sleep, fatigue or loss of energy, loss of ability to concentrate or make decisions, decreased sexual drive, and recurrent thoughts of death.

DSM-IV, recognizing this as a potential problem, states that
symptoms should not be due to the "direct physiological effects of a
substance or a general medical condition." In addition, some symptoms, such as "thoughts about death," are absolutely normal when
a person is dying. One might go further and say that the lack of such
thoughts is abnormal. Moreover, thoughts of suicide are what has
brought this person to you in the first place; he is requesting your
help in ending his life.

If DSM-IV is of little use here, where do you go? You might start
with a variation of the manual's checklist and a review of the patient's medical history. For example, you might ask the patient
about his thoughts, his sleeping patterns, the pleasure he obtains
from the activities he can still physically engage in, the behavioral
or social patterns that have not been affected by his physical symptoms, his ability to think clearly, concentrate, and make decisions,
and his emotional outlook. You might ask, for example:

- "What do you think about, most of the time? Recently, what's
  been concerning you the most?"

- "Are you having difficulty sleeping? What's keeping you awake? What do you think about?"

- "Do you find any small pleasures in life? Do you still engage in any favorite activities?"

- "How do you feel, emotionally, right now?"

The types of questions you ask will, of course, be dependent on the patient's physical condition, prognosis, and proximity to death. The following is an example.

CLINICIAN: Do you have any interests or hobbies? Do you have anything that still brings you pleasure?

PATIENT: Not really.

CLINICIAN: Before you got sick, what did you do for fun? Did you have any hobbies or special activities?

PATIENT: I used to go hiking, but obviously, I don't have the energy for it anymore. Or I'd get together with friends. The usual. That's about it.

CLINICIAN: You can drive. Do you still get out, or get together with your friends?

PATIENT: Someone will visit once in a while, or call. But I don't go out. I don't really like to see anyone.

CLINICIAN: Is there any particular reason?

PATIENT: I just don't feel like it. I don't feel like I fit in anymore.

CLINICIAN: Fit in? Where, with your friends?

PATIENT: No. Anywhere. Everywhere I go reminds me that people have lives and futures. I don't. I'd rather be alone.

A preliminary discussion such as this may or may not provide you with the clues you need to determine the appropriateness of a patient's request. You might do well to review any background information you already have, and then

- Review your past conversations and experience with the patient for any historical evidence of depression or other psychiatric condition

- Review past conversations for changes in patterns of communication and for signs of withdrawal

- Check the possible side effects of the medications and treatments the patient is receiving for the likelihood of depression

- Search the patient's file for any indication of prior psychiatric conditions, prescriptions for mood-altering or antidepressant medications, substance abuse, suicide attempts, or family history that includes a suicide

- Look for nonverbal signs of a depressed mood—for example, in facial expressions and demeanor

- Notice any physical agitation or retardation in speech and movement that would not be expected given the patient's physical illness and prescribed medication

Historical evidence of a depressive episode or the possibility of side effects from current medications should not in themselves cast doubt on the thoughtfulness of a patient's current request for help. His request should not be dismissed merely because he once experienced or was once diagnosed with a mood disorder. The immediate call is for validation of his feelings and needs as he perceives them. If you have any doubts about the rationality of the patient's request, I would again recommend obtaining his permission to seek a more in-depth assessment from a mental health professional.

"Rational Death"

The dilemma of rational suicide has long been debated in the mental health literature, and a number of elements have been identified as indicating rationality in the decision. Although the analysis has tended to focus on suicide in the general population, some attention has been given to cases involving life-threatening or terminal illness.

After conducting a number of surveys of psychotherapists' attitudes to suicide, James Werth and Debra Cobia compiled a list of "criteria for rational suicide." Their list suggests that the patient

- Not make the decision impulsively but consider all alternatives
- Make the decision freely, without coercion
- Consider the congruence of the act with her personal values
- Consider the impact of the act on significant others

Werth also stresses the need for a mental health professional to make an assessment of mental competence. To be viewed as competent, he says, a patient should be able to

- Understand and remember the information relevant to the decision that is to be made
- Appreciate the consequences of the decision
- Have an underlying set of values that provides some guidance in decision making
- Communicate the decision and explain the process used

In Chapter Four, where I will be talking about the involvement of family in the decision process, I will discuss the issues of coercion and effects on others. But here I will address the question of assessing the congruence of action and values.

Listening for Contradictory Values

Like Werth and Cobia, I believe that one of the signs that renders the rationality of a patient's request suspect is an apparent lack of congruence between actions and values. In this context, values can refer to a patient's general philosophy of life, personal goals and interests, previously expressed attitudes about end-of-life care, and moral and spiritual beliefs.

You might begin by listening closely for a possible contradiction of values within the patient's request itself or in the reasons she states for wanting your help. Also be alert to possible contradictory motives, such as loss of connection with others and a desire to make an autonomous decision. Similarly, as I will describe in detail in Chapter Four, a patient may talk of her belief in family and open communication but be unwilling to share her plans with those close to her. These may or may not be contradictions, and they need to be looked at further. They may point to possible conflict or depression, both of which should be explored.

You might also look for significant changes in a patient's expressed goals and interests. A man who previously has said, "I want to live until Christmas" or "I want to live until I can see my brother" or "I want to live to attend my daughter's graduation" should be questioned about his sudden change of plans, especially in the absence of major changes in his physical condition or quality of life. You might obtain such information by asking:

- "Until recently, was there anything you had been looking forward to?"
- "Is anything of importance happening in the weeks or months ahead that you might miss?"
- "Are there any friends or family members you planned to see?"
- "Is there anything you still want to accomplish, or do, before you die?"

Once it becomes obvious that a conflict exists, you might question why the goal or desire is no longer important. The patient may well have a valid reason for this change of plans. Or the change may be suggestive of depression and feelings of hopelessness or worthlessness.

You also might search for significant changes in the patient's stated attitudes about end-of-life care. You can draw on your own memory of conversations you have had with the patient or check his file for information about "do not resuscitate" orders, living wills, health care proxies, or other advance directives for decision making.

If no information is present, you would do well to ask the patient a few questions about this. Again, the answers may give you an idea of the possible conflict between the current request and previously held attitudes about care.

Finally, you might see conflict of values in the patient's expressed desire to die and his spiritual beliefs. Devout members of certain religious denominations might not be expected to request aid in dying, let alone support it. Nevertheless, church membership and attendance in themselves cannot always be correlated with a conflict of values. People attend churches for various reasons and do not always staunchly support the official dogma. If in doubt, you might ask the patient questions about his religious and spiritual perspectives on assisted dying.

Questions to Ask Yourself

A patient's request for your help offers a perfect opportunity to test your skills in communicating, in asking the right questions, and in making a proper assessment. As I have said before, a request usually comes without warning and can stimulate various reactions. Regardless of your experience with such requests, I recommend that you create this scenario in your imagination and practice an initial assessment. You might ask yourself:

- Has the patient given me any indication of the seriousness of her request?
- Has she expressed interest in ending her life soon, or has she indicated that this is but one of many options, and that she sees it as insurance for the future?
- Has she outlined any specific rationale for wanting to consider this option?
- Have there been any recent changes in her physical condition or quality of life that I have not yet had the opportunity to discuss with her?

- Am I aware of any changes in her economic situation, or social or home environment, that may be influencing this decision?

- Have there been any recent changes in her treatment? Might there be new treatment-based stressors, or medications with known mood-altering side effects?

- Have my previous conversations with her, or her advance directives ("do not resuscitate" orders, living wills, or health care proxies), indicated that this request was forthcoming?

- Do I believe the request—and the rationale provided—is appropriate in this case, given the patient's condition, prognosis, and apparent quality of life? If so, why?

- What personal assumptions about suffering and quality of life am I relying on in making this determination?

- What underlying factors, special concerns, or fears might be influencing this patient's decision?

- Am I absolutely certain that the patient is rational and competent, and not influenced by depression or overwhelming despair?

*****

Working with patients at this time in their lives, when they have every reason to be in despair, is a learned skill. The patient who has come to you with a request for aid in dying is in an extremely vulnerable position. It most likely took significant thought and emotional preparation for her to finally request your help. For whatever reason, this person has placed herself at your mercy. Nevertheless, all of the fears that may be motivating her desire to die may be nothing at this moment compared to her fear of being rejected by you—of not only being turned down but being made to feel weak in character. Know this, show your concern, and provide a level of emotional support with which you and your patient feel most comfortable.

You have a choice in how you will define your relationship with your patient. On hearing her request, you can stand back and increase the emotional distance, you can empathize to the point of ignoring your own personal and professional needs, or you can be supportive while seeking to learn as much as you can about the patient's decision.

You may feel uncomfortable talking about motives and feelings, especially with a patient who is likely to die. But such talk is critical. It helps you get to know the patient, and also can act as a form of healing. For just being with the patient and allowing her to talk about these issues shows your concern and compassion. Your role is that of a caring inquisitor whose interest is in the depths of the patient's soul.

It may take some time before your patient is willing to talk openly. You should not force her to do so. On the other hand, you should understand that her request for help entitles you to ask certain questions, including some she may not feel comfortable answering.

I would add that you need to keep your own counsel and avoid falling into agreement with the patient's motives and thinking processes. A patient's desperation can be contagious and is best countered by maintaining a calm, professional, supportive attitude. This benefits both you and your patient. Further, as I have attempted to show throughout this chapter, you must always remember that you may not have heard the whole story. (I will address this point in more detail in Chapter Four.) Also bear in mind that the desperation a patient may feel is often temporary and may even lift somewhat, simply as a result of talking with you and receiving your validation. Finally, although pharmacology should not be viewed as a panacea for all the ills of a patient's soul, remember that depression can frequently be treated and overcome by appropriate combinations of medication and counseling.

Through compassion and open communication, you may learn a patient's innermost language and come to understand her motives for seeking an end to life. But you may also help her better understand herself. Thus, if she continues on her journey, she may be better prepared to make her choices with wisdom.

I believe in the power of communication—in patients, clinicians, and family members being able to freely discuss their most important concerns. But I also know that not all are adept at doing this, or indeed want to. With any particular patient, it may not be possible for you to open the necessary dialogue. Nevertheless, you should make the attempt to do so. If you are to reach a decision that is based on wisdom, you must understand as much as you can about this person, including her relationships with her family and significant others. As the issues involving family and assisted dying are complex, I will address them in detail in a separate chapter, which follows.

4

Understanding Family Dynamics

Some clinicians seem to forget that patients are more than biological entities, that they also have personal lives that transcend illness, medical treatment, and the prospect of death. Patients—ill and alone and in need of treatment—do not materialize out of nowhere. They are born as mostly healthy beings who are dependent on their families, they develop as individuals within families, and live in families for much, if not most, of their lives. Some patients, it is true, are totally alone, but most are part of a family of some kind, to which they are connected by blood, marriage, or emotion. In marriage, they may have expanded their blood lines. And even if blood ties are gone, by death or by choice, there may still be a "family" to which the patient is attached, in her heart and in practice. Patients often have created families out of friendship, to fill the void that exists between themselves and the larger world.

You may know your patient only as she exists in your office or in the hospital. You may be aware of her connections to others only from the family medical history in her file or from the portrait she has painted of others by her words. You may have met a partner, family member, or other significant relation during the course of treating her, but you may have paid little attention to that person. The home life of this patient, may, in all likelihood, exist for you as a closed and remote world.

Although the clinician-patient relationship is one that typically binds you to the patient alone, a fuller understanding of her choices and motives requires that you grasp her as an individual within a web of connection to others. If a patient requests your help in dying, it is critical to obtain a picture of the life she has led outside the confines of illness. Regardless of your position on the issue of assisted suicide, such knowledge can help you uncover and understand the larger dynamics that may be motivating her. Among other things, you might learn about

- Interpersonal conflicts between the patient and her significant relations
- Withdrawal from significant relations, feelings of hopelessness and other signs of depression, or evidence of alcohol or substance abuse
- Previous emotional trauma or significant losses
- Psychosocial and economic stressors within the home, or "coercion" by others in the patient's decision

Such knowledge of the patient's home life and relations can provide you with important clues about her underlying motives and decision-making processes. For example, how might difficulties communicating the presence of unresolved interpersonal issues, a history of significant loss or emotional trauma, or other stressors within the patient's home or larger family intensify her difficulty in dealing with the trauma of illness? And how might any of these factors affect her decision to end her life?

Knowledge of family connections is also critical for understanding the possible effects—on the patient's significant others and on yourself—of helping her die. Although your responsibility is to this one person, her life and death are important elements in the lives of others. Not only is she a patient receiving your medical care, nursing support, or counseling, she is also a spouse or partner, a daughter, a mother, a sister, or a friend, and she is part of a larger community. In requesting your help in dying, she is also asking you to help sever these connections and everything they represent for others in the larger web.

Without obtaining a picture of the patient within her larger environment, you will not be able to discern whether she is requesting your help, in part, because of

- Feelings of alienation from the family, a sense of isolation, and a lack of belonging

- A desire to relieve significant others of the perceived burden of care

- Feelings of anger or resentment toward her family or a family member

- A lack of willingness on the part of significant relations to discuss her career as a patient or the intolerable nature of her suffering

- Preexisting emotional pain and suffering that others have failed to address

There may be many other feelings and factors underlying a request. Patients commonly feel conflicted between wanting to meet their own needs by ending their lives and wanting to please, meet the needs of, or avoid hurting their significant relations. I have heard many with terminal or life-changing conditions say they feel trapped by their commitments to others. They might say, "If I didn't have children, and if I didn't worry so much about hurting them, I'd leave right now" or "At times, I feel like they weigh me down, and just wish they'd get out of the way."

Similarly, there may be confusion or anger if the patient believes that others are selfishly ignoring the seriousness of her condition, her suffering, or her desires because they are unwilling to let her go and allow her to die. Such feelings may be expressed in comments like "They don't understand how bad I feel," "They refuse to see that I'm dying," and "They keep trying to hold on, though I'm ready to go."

UNCOVERING PATIENT–FAMILY CONFLICT

Not all families or home environments exist as sanctuaries for the expression of emotional support for their members. Instead, the patient's home may be a center of emotional neglect, where individual need and personal choice receive no recognition. The home may be dominated by one person, or it may resemble a war zone where conflict and rebellion are accepted features of everyday life. In the worst case, there may be patterns of physical or verbal violence or other forms of abuse, and the patient may have been either a victim or a perpetrator of such acts. It is also possible that a patient's illness has added to preexisting tension. In some cases, it may serve as the "last straw" that breaks a family's capacity to remain emotionally functional. In other instances, it may bring underlying issues to the surface and provide the opportunity for their resolution.

In such family environments, prevailing patterns of interaction and conflict may increase the emotional burden or sense of isolation felt by a patient. It is imperative, therefore, that you assess the potential influence of such factors on the patient's decision. Without doing so, you cannot know whether you are responding to the symptoms of problems other than those engendered by the illness.

In other cases, the patient's connection with his disturbed family environment may have been severed long ago, and he may now feel very much alone, but without any desire to reestablish contact or to obtain any sense of closure. Alternatively, your patient may have experienced a divorce or the death of a significant relation and may subsequently have moved to another city where he has few ties and, seemingly, nowhere to turn for emotional support. Or there may be a history of suicide in a patient's family that predisposes him to end his own life during the trauma of his illness.

To attempt to uncover such problems, you would do well to ask the patient whether he has discussed his desire to die with his family members or other significant relations, and if so, in what degree of detail. The practical value of his answer will, of course, depend on how much you already know about the basic structure of his home environment and primary relationships. If you are a physician or nursing professional and have worked with him for some time, you may be somewhat aware of this background and may even have met a partner, family member, or other significant person during an office visit. If you are a hospice nurse or social worker, you are probably more aware than others of the patient's home life and any problems associated with it. And if you are a therapist or family counselor, you may have focused on such concerns for some time and may be working on them with your client and the person who is most involved.

Assuming that your knowledge of the patient's home background is sketchy, it is critical to obtain as much information as you can about his current home life, his primary relationships, and his ties to biological family. You might begin by asking:

- "Do you have a spouse or partner or other primary relationship? If so, what is the status of that relationship?"

- "If you do not have a primary relationship, do you have a singularly important relationship with another person, such as a child, sibling, parent, or close friend?"

- "Tell me about your home life. Do you live with family members or a partner?"

- "Who is your primary caregiver?

- "Tell me about your family. Do you have children, siblings, parents?"

- "Have you maintained ties to members of your family, former partners, or people with whom you've had significant relationships?"

- "If so, do you give each other emotional or practical support? Do you visit, call, or write each other?"

- "Have you called on any of these people for help during your illness? Could you call on them if you needed to do so? If not, why not?"

- "If you do not have relationships with a partner or family member, do you have a close friendship network or ties to others through a church or other organization?"

Problems in Communication

Some of the difficulties a patient faces may relate to problems in communication with her significant other—problems you may not be aware of because they do not surface when the patient is communicating with you. Although she may be capable of asking for your help in ending her life, she may not feel sufficient comfort or emotional safety to discuss these same issues with her significant relations. Of course, the reverse is also possible: the patient may bring her request to you with great difficulty long after she has held serious discussions with others.

Patients and members of their significant circle may not know how to communicate in positive ways with each other or to express the full range of their thoughts, opinions, and heartfelt feelings. They may find it easier to resort to withdrawal or silence, confrontational outbursts, passive-aggressive communication, or other potentially negative interaction patterns. What is left unsaid may far outweigh anything spoken.

Even when significant relations do provide a level of emotional support, they may still lack the skills to discuss topics they consider negative or threatening, such as a patient's illness and the likelihood of death.

Further, some patients—influenced, perhaps by their cultural or family background—have a tendency to rely on nonverbal means to convey their feelings. They may have some reason to expect that others will understand these messages, or they may simply feel that the verbal expression of weakness, confusion, physical pain and suffering, or independence of thought exposes them to risk.

Whatever the dominant pattern of communication between a patient and her significant relations, it cannot be considered effective if it does not allow her to express her thoughts and feelings and receive validation and support. Improvement in such a pattern can be achieved only by concerted effort on the part of the individuals involved, possibly with professional help.

Unsatisfactory patterns of communication may reflect genuine and serious difficulties a patient may have with her family or significant relations. And these may affect her feelings about illness and the possibility of premature death, as well as her final choices. It is therefore critical that you at least make an attempt to uncover such problems. At the time of a patient's initial request, you might ask a series of questions about communication patterns within her family or household. For example:

- "Do your family members or other significant relations know how you feel? Do they know what you'd like to do? Have you specifically talked with them about assisted suicide?"

- "If not, have you discussed with them the possibility or likelihood of your death?"

- "Have you talked with anyone else—a friend, therapist, or other health professional—about your possible death or your thoughts of assisted suicide?"

- "Do you anticipate sharing your plans about assisted suicide with your family or other significant relations?"

- "Do members of your family, or other significant relations, support your decision? Do they support it fully? Do they agree with the reasons for your decision and with your choice of timing?"

- "Are you typically open with your family and significant relations? When something is bothering any of you, do you openly share your concerns with each other?"

- "Would you say that you and your family members or significant relations mutually support each other? How is this support expressed?"

Values and Conflict Revisited

As I pointed out in Chapter Three, one way to assess the rationality of a patient's decision to die is to look for an apparent conflict of values, as expressed in the patient's words, expressed motives, and planned behavior. In this context, *values* refers to a patient's philosophy of life, personal goals and interests, previously expressed attitudes about end-of-life care, and basic moral and spiritual beliefs.

Besides its utility in assessing rationality, the search for a potential conflict of motives can also uncover disharmony within the patient's family or home environment with respect to the decision. It can, further, reveal problems that the patient and his significant relations are having in communicating their needs to each other or in deliberating on the best course of action.

As before, you might begin by listening closely for a possible contradiction of values in the request itself or in the reasons the patient gives for wanting your help. For example, the patient may say, "I love my family and wouldn't want to hurt them," but then admit to having "no plans" to talk with them about the decision. One possibility is that he believes that any prior discussion of his plans would be more wrenching for the family than no discussion at all. Another is that he does not care about hurting them or sees no need to prepare them emotionally for his death or to give them opportunities to share their own concerns.

On the surface, this might appear to be an obvious conflict, and possibly even "irrational." Indeed, the move toward secrecy and toward cutting significant relations out of this most important decision may be a sign of withdrawal and depression. And if there are serious problems within the family or household, the decision may also be a means for the patient to escape, express anger, or relieve others of the burden of his care.

A policy of secrecy may also suggest current friction within the family about the decision. The patient may have brought up the topic, only to have it rejected, and he may have decided to pursue his chosen course of action nevertheless. "Love of family" and the pursuit of "freedom and autonomy" may both be important to him, but the latter is taking precedence in the extreme conditions of suffering he is enduring. Alternatively, "openness and honesty" may be less significant in this family than a sense of "independence."

Secrecy may also be a device that is characteristic of the relationship between the patient and his family. Perhaps he has always seen himself as somehow separate from and independent of others and has engaged in secrecy at various times throughout his life. Or members of his family may have frequently withheld information from him.

You might check on the possible conflict in values by asking the patient about his style of communication with his family and significant relations and about his concerns for their feelings and for the effects of his actions. Such questions might include:

- "What is more important to you, your family or your independence? Do you see any conflict between what you value and what you plan to do?"

- "Do you worry about how your death might affect members of your family or other significant relations? Have you taken their needs into consideration?"

- "Do you have a clear idea of how they might react to your assisted death?"

- "Do you think they have the right to know how you feel, and what you're planning to do?"

As a clinician, you will feel comfortable with a decision to help only if you are comfortable with the patient's decision, and this implies an acceptance of the values he has brought to bear on the issue. If family, openness, and the opportunity for closure are important to you, you will probably feel more at ease in helping a person die if his decision reflects those values. As in all aspects of assisted suicide, you are obliged to make a close examination of underlying motives.

WHEN FAMILIES ARE NOT INFORMED

Patients often claim that they are keeping their plans secret to protect themselves or others. Obviously, there are more complex reasons, but most explanations seem to begin here. In either case, you would do well to explore such reasons in detail.

Protecting Oneself

There are those who claim that their secrecy is needed to protect themselves from unwanted intrusion from family members or others. For example, one man with AIDS who said he had been "promised a prescription" by his psychiatrist but had no immediate desire to end his life, said he could not tell his family his plans because "they'd intervene" to stop him. He explained: "I know them. They'd pull out all the stops and notify the authorities."

He said the issue was one of personal choice, and this wasn't the only important secret he'd kept from his family over the years. The first secret was his being gay. The second was his being HIV-positive. Although necessity finally forced him to share these facts, he said that he had for years kept his sexual preference secret "not to protect them, but to keep them from interfering" in his life. He explained that he had learned early on in childhood to "agree with everything they had to say, and not make waves." Otherwise, discussions would escalate into arguments he could never win. For him, concealment became a form of winning. He saw his current emphasis on secrecy as something the family communication pattern required.

In addition to this apparently "reasonable" explanation—fear of intervention and loss of autonomy—there are other motives for secrecy that you may find far less reasonable. For example, a patient may desire to protect himself from

- Descending into emotion, facing his losses, and assessing his life
- Dealing with unfinished emotional business with his family
- Losing his personal philosophy, view of the world, or sense of certainty about ending his life

As I mentioned in Chapter Three, it is not unusual for a patient to desire escape from all the emotional debris— disappointment, regret, grief, and guilt—that has accumulated over a lifetime and never been fully addressed. We may all, at some level, be ambivalent about facing such feelings, sharing them with others, and emotionally completing the business of life. Although the period before death is, for some, a time for personal assessment, righting wrongs, and facing, letting go, and recovering from old pain, not everyone welcomes this chastening review.

I have seen both types of individual make the decision to seek an assisted death. This is not a choice made solely by escapists. Similarly, I have seen both make the decision to include or exclude others from their plans to end their lives. Nevertheless, I cannot help but find suspect those who maintain secrecy to avoid the final work of life: descent into emotion, confrontation of losses, closure of relationships.

Some individuals, of course, see no positive value in disclosing their intentions concerning assisted death and attempting to resolve past wrongs. For them, closure is something to be achieved within themselves, out of necessity, when they accept the circumstances of their life and the fact that others may never change. As one woman told me:

I have no desire to ever see my father again. I couldn't possibly confront him about the abuse, the incest, and his alcoholism, because it's still there. It might let me vent my anger, but I'd have to spend valuable time and energy dredging up things better left alone. . . . I've accepted the situation and myself, and that's enough. I don't have much time, and what time I have left I want to spend in peace.

More suspect are those who decide to exclude significant relations from their decision out of fear that they will be talked out of their beliefs concerning assisted dying. This can be seen in the following dialogue with a breast cancer patient, where it is obvious there are additional suspect motives.

CLINICIAN: How do you feel about this decision?

PATIENT: Wrung out, I guess. I'm sad it's come to this, but I'm exhausted. I don't want to die, but I don't want to stay. . . . It's become too much. I just want an easier path if it gets worse.

CLINICIAN: Does your husband know how you feel? Does he know what you'd like to do?

PATIENT: No. I can't talk with him about this. Not now. Maybe later.

CLINICIAN: You don't think he'd support this?

PATIENT: No. It's not that. If I told him, we'd have to talk about the cancer, and my dying. We might have to talk about feelings.

CLINICIAN: Who would this be a problem for, you or him?

PATIENT: Him, primarily. He doesn't want to hear about me dying, or being sad or exhausted. None of us can talk about death, or anything negative. . . . I think my illness makes him feel helpless that he can't do anything, and that he's not in control.

CLINICIAN: And how does that make you feel?

PATIENT: Like I'm choking on all this. Here I am, dying. I'm losing myself, yet I can't even talk about it.

CLINICIAN: You're talking now. That's a start.

PATIENT: Yeah, but I'm not talking with him, am I?

CLINICIAN: And if you did talk with him, especially about your decision?

PATIENT: He'd talk me out of it, and I wouldn't want that.

Protecting Others

Some patients have told me that their secrecy is needed to protect others. "It's really for their own good," one man said. "It would hurt them too much." Another explained that his Roman Catholic mother would be "devastated" if she knew his plans. The religious considerations, which no longer bothered him, "would destroy her. . . . She'd consider it suicide, and think I'd go to hell for it. It's bad enough I'm dying. Why add to her grief?" Both of these men said they would wait as long as they could, within the bounds of safety, and then make sure that their deaths appeared to be due to natural causes, thereby further protecting their families from the truth.

Secrecy can be maintained to protect others not just from emotional pain but from

- The economic and practical burden of caring for them
- The moral quandary of keeping the true cause and the assisted nature of the death secret from emotionally vulnerable family members or others
- The grief of having to face the patient's final agonizing process of dying
- Descending into their own emotional debris

Information about a planned assisted death is often shared selectively. As a result, families may be split into those who know and those who don't. This can create a moral quandary for those who know, interfere with their grieving process, and require them to maintain constant self-censorship. Yet the risk remains that the secret will accidentally be revealed to uninformed family members or others.

Some of this protection may well be altruistic, but it can equally be self-serving, its real aim being the protection of patients from their own emotions, their own grief, and their own perception of an agonizing dying process and the difficulties they might have in resolving unfinished business with others.

Secrecy and Confidentiality

When a patient explains her secrecy in terms of protection of self or others, your suspicions should be raised. In either case, it is likely that she is failing to take into account the potential impact of her assisted death on others. You might also be concerned about the possibility that her family or significant relations have information about her that would be of critical use to you in your evaluation. Without the patient's permission for you to talk with them about her desires, the ethics of patient confidentiality prevent you from fully accessing this potentially valuable resource.

Nevertheless, some information on a patient's home and family life can be obtained without breaching confidentiality. For example, if the patient is in a primary relationship or has family members with whom she lives or has ties, I would recommend that you

- Ask her to invite her significant others to a consultation on various nonconfidential aspects of the case, including elements of care and any concerns that these individuals might have
- Suggest that she seek counseling with a trusted mental health professional who might be willing to assess for you the patient's current psychological and mental status

- Recommend that she participate in family or couple counseling with a significant family member or relation

- Contact a representative of her hospice care team (if she has been referred to hospice) to discuss her home and family situation and her psychosocial status

- Request that the hospice team directly contact you (rather than other staff members in your office) with any updates on the patient's care, home situation, and psychosocial status

WHEN FAMILIES KNOW

When a patient is honest with his family and significant relations about his desire to end his life, the response may be complete acceptance, hesitant support, or outright opposition. You need to know, however, that any one of these outcomes may be associated with difficulties. Neither endorsement nor opposition can be taken as a definitive indicator of the quality of the patient's significant relationships. Manipulative and hostile families can be found at both ends of the spectrum, and so can loving and supportive ones.

The rigidity of a family's religious beliefs may play a role in opposition, but so too may an unwillingness on the part of significant others to give up hope, even in the face of great suffering and imminent death. On the other hand, those who support a patient's decision include those who compassionately empathize with his suffering, others who arrive at their position on more philosophical grounds, and even some whose support arises from their physical or emotional exhaustion as caregivers. Personal self-interest can also play a role. No position holds a monopoly on virtue.

It is clear from the cases with which I have been familiar that neither position is ever easy to hold, and few significant relations hold their position without some doubts—both before and after the patient's death. For many families who agree with the patient's decision, an assisted death is seen as the lesser evil; the greater evil would be to allow the person's suffering to continue unchecked, particularly given the strength of the person's desire to die. But many who oppose such actions use similar terms, seeing assisted suicide as the greater evil. The difference between these positions is not necessarily rooted in morality but in a view of what is and is not an acceptable option in a particular circumstance. For some, anything that approximates "suicide" or "killing" is always unacceptable. For others, intolerable suffering is unacceptable, especially when merciful relief might possibly be achieved through an assisted death.

Families and significant relations can be extremely vulnerable to the effects of a patient's illness. Along with the patient himself, they may feel utterly stripped of power by the terminal or life-changing condition. It is not easy to watch a person with whom one has shared a life deteriorate toward death, not easy to stand by as this person changes physically, mentally, emotionally, and socially before one's eyes. The sense of inadequacy may be overwhelming. This is especially the case for caregivers, who are companions in the patient's emotional journey throughout his illness. They may make their own descent into the troubling past, with all of its incompleteness and regret. Love, anxiety, frustration—every type of emotion may be experienced during this time, and expressed in both positive and negative ways.

It is into this cauldron of emotion that a patient's statements about assisted dying fall. And as I have mentioned before, such statements may be susceptible to a variety of interpretations, each with its own emotional consequences for those hearing them. The expression of a desire to die may, of course, be just what it appears to be: the result of a thoughtful process of deliberation, ending in certainty, which the patient now wishes to share. But patients may initiate the discussion of assisted death with any of a number of conscious or unconscious goals:

- To express their discontent with their illness and convince others of their absolute physical misery

- To shock their significant relations into understanding the depth of their despair

- To secure proof that others are listening and receive assurance that their lives still have value

- To punish or hurt family members and significant others by announcing a choice these individuals are sure to oppose

It is because of the possibility of such less-than-positive motives that your understanding of the patient's family dynamics is vital. Therefore, you need to do more than just ask a patient, "Does your family know of your desires?" and "Do they support your decision?" Although such knowledge and support are often positive signs that the patient has considered the complexity of the issue and has taken into account the possible effects of his action on others, they do not tell you the complete story. They do not indicate, for example, the depth of support provided by others, their knowledge of possible treatment alternatives, their own motives, or whether they have thoroughly assessed the quality of the patient's decision.

When Others Agree

There is no one primary reason why some families and significant relations, either fully or hesitantly, support a patient's desire to die. Their reasons often mirror the patient's own expressed motives, especially the desire for mercy in the face of intolerable suffering.

Those who support patients' decisions arrive at this point along different paths. From my own observation, most make up their minds on the basis of loving empathy with the patient's physical and emotional suffering. One of their struggles, of course, is to balance the patient's need to die with their own tenacious hopes for a miracle cure, recovery, or remission. Only after a harrowing review of probabilities may they conclude that there is no reasonable alternative. Ultimately, their agreement may reflect a mixture of thoughtful reflection and deeply felt emotion.

Typically, when a patient is in a close relationship, the decision to seek help in dying is not made unilaterally. Rather, it may involve both parties in a subtle dance, the patient gradually convincing the caregiver of his personal philosophy and of the need for such an action. Each party—alone or together—may weigh the pros and cons of an assisted death. Eventually, the other person may become a strong supporter, even to the extent of exploring on her own the intricacies of assisted dying.

Some agree with the decision only after long discussion. Others, however, may find themselves with little time to discuss and think about the issue. In certain instances, significant others may be forced to rapidly shift their position, especially when the patient's demands and physical suffering can no longer be ignored. Increased pain or the development of new, unacceptable, or threatening symptoms may force hesitant family members or other relations into reluctant agreement. The overwhelming case for mercy, combined with their own feelings of helplessness, makes further resistance impossible.

The agreement of some may be grounded in a philosophy of life and death that they have previously shared with the patient. They may have little difficulty agreeing when the patient's physical condition deteriorates to a point they have previously defined as intolerable.

Others agree not so much out of commitment to principle as out of a sense of duty to the person. They may see the need to stand by their dying partner or family member whatever that individual decides, because they long ago promised to do so, or because this is what is expected of them as a dutiful partner or child. One woman who helped her husband die told me: "I was his wife, and he believed in this. Of course I supported him." Another said: "He was my husband and closest friend, and he wanted this so badly. I didn't want to lose him, but wasn't going to fight him now."

There are many other possible reasons for agreeing. Family members or significant others may be exhausted from caregiving. They may be worn down by a patient's adamant statements of desire.

They may want, more than anything, to please the person they love. Or they may be intimidated by other family members who are more verbal, powerful, or respected. Such motives may well reflect their characteristic, lifelong pattern of behavior and decision making.

It goes without saying that when families and significant others agree to a patient's plan, they are not necessarily fully informed of the alternatives, especially for pain relief and other forms of palliative care. They may have little knowledge of hospice services, or even of available health benefits. Choices for final care are much broader than hospitalization and invasive life-sustaining procedures, yet families may not know this. They may not appreciate, either, that nursing care is not restricted to convalescent facilities—or that those facilities themselves are often far better than a patient might imagine.

Many family members and significant others, conscious of their lack of knowledge and feeling excluded from the clinician-patient relationship anyway, allow the patient to be the final arbiter of her condition, treatment plans, and ultimate fate. In some of these instances, they may all too willingly agree with her chosen solution.

Assessing the Nature of Family Agreement

It is critical that you understand both the evolution of the patient's decision and the evolution and nature of the claimed support by others. Even when a patient seems firm in his request for your help, he may still be influenced by his close circle. Or he may be obscuring the fact that the support of his significant others is lukewarm or a result of his own insistent demands. There may be real or potential opposition that he has failed to describe.

If the patient appears to meet your personal criteria, and you are tempted to help, one possible solution is to request a meeting with the patient's partner or other significant relation to discuss the situation. If the patient refuses on the basis of confidentiality, you must honor this, but you also need to ask for the specific reasons behind such a refusal, given the patient's claim that others support him.

In suggesting such a meeting, you should make clear to the patient that the purpose is not to make any final decision about assisting in his death but to discuss a full range of concerns. This discussion can assist you in several ways. It can provide you with additional information about the patient's condition and general attitude, which will be helpful in understanding his problems and unmet treatment needs. It can also serve as an opportunity to talk about future treatment options and hospice care and to assess the need of respite for current caregivers.

It is one thing to hear from a patient, "My children see it my way." It is another to talk with the children themselves and discover that their support bobs on a sea of ambivalence. This can be seen in the following dialogue:

CLINICIAN: Your father has said that you support his decision. Is that right?

SON: We all hate to see him suffer.

CLINICIAN: Do you think this is the right decision?

SON: He seems to think so. If this is what he wants, I wouldn't stand in his way.

CLINICIAN: But do you support this? Is the time right?

SON: I'd like to see him stick around longer, if that's what you mean. But this is his decision, not mine.

CLINICIAN: What does the rest of the family think?

SON: We're not gung ho. There's no consensus. My sister doesn't really want to talk about it. She gets angry. She's said, "Maybe down the line, if he gets bad and nothing else can be done." But she'd like him around for a while. She's got kids, and hasn't had enough of him yet.

CLINICIAN: Have you?

SON: Have I had enough of him? Sometimes. He can be a pain and get on your nerves. He's worse now, but he's always been like that to some degree. You get used to it. We all love him. We ignore it.

It may be easier to hold such a discussion if you are a therapist or a member of a hospice team. Under those circumstances, a framework for this type of dialogue already exists, and both you and the significant other will see it as clearly a part of your function. If you are a physician, on the other hand, such a conversation may be difficult to initiate, both because it is not traditionally associated with your role and because you have many competing demands on your time. If it is to happen, it will require a commitment on your part to work for the best interests of your patient, whatever that takes.

Moreover, as a clinician, you may feel that you are taking a significant risk in talking about this topic, no matter what you finally decide to do. And if you later agree to help the patient, you may fear that your involvement will be obvious to those with whom you have met.

What you need to believe is that the benefits of such a meeting, in terms of information on a wide range of patient care issues, far outweigh the risks of talking about assisted death. As one physician told me, "Over the years, I've come to realize that I learn more about a patient's symptoms from listening to a husband or wife." There is much truth in this, for the patient may well be nervous and forgetful during an appointment, or may focus only on his most obvious or current concern.

I have talked with several clinicians who explained how their thoughts about a patient and assisted suicide were sometimes reversed or the request was taken much more seriously as a result of such a meeting. One physician told me:

> When you see a terminal patient in the company of an anxious husband or wife, and there's obvious love and concern, and the patient is talking about wanting to die, and you stop talking about symptoms and treatment and start talking about feelings, you can't help but think about the importance of your role and what all of this is doing to the spouse. You can't ignore it.

Similarly, an oncologist stated that when he met the husband of a breast cancer patient, "Her request became real, as she became more than a patient." As a result, his concern for her deepened. And an internist with a large HIV practice related that in one case,

> Seeing the obvious love between these two men, who came together to every appointment, ended all my questions. When my patient finally asked for my help, and his partner just firmly nodded, I knew I had to help. There was absolute certainty in their faces, which took away my hesitation.

The questions you might ask a patient's partner or significant other in such a meeting should cover a few basic points:

- "Do you think this is the right decision under the circumstances? Are you absolutely certain about this? What convinced you? Have you thought about alternatives?"
- "Why do you think he wants to do this? Is there anything else going on in his life that might be influencing his decision?"
- "How long has he been talking about this? How soon do you think he would do it?"
- "What has his state of mind been like lately? Has he been depressed or down more than in the past?"
- "Is his mind made up? Do you think he is absolutely certain about this decision? Has he thought about any alternatives?"
- "Are you the primary person caring for him? How has this been? Have you been able to get enough rest? Is anyone else helping you?"
- "What do others in the family think about this? Do they all know? Has he let others tell him what they think? Does everyone support his decision?"

Whether to meet with a significant relation alone or in the presence of the patient is a judgment call; there is much to be gained or lost either way. If you are not a trained therapist, the presence of the patient may make it difficult for you to ask some of these questions. You might also assume that the patient's presence may affect the honesty of your interviewee, but this is not necessarily the case. In fact, your questions may stimulate a dialogue that you find instructive.

However the discussion is structured, you need to make sure that it does not become a wedge between the patient and the significant relation and does not make the patient feel marginalized or isolated in any way. Further, you must avoid taking sides, confronting the patient, or making any negative comments about the patient's desires. The perspectives of both parties are based on feelings that are valid to them. And remember, your primary relationship is with the patient, not the other person.

When Others Disagree

In some cases, the patient under your care will lack support for his decision from his partner, his family, a single family member, or some other significant relation. Suffering intolerably, he is certain of his decision, which is the result of long and thoughtful consideration. Yet his desires, philosophy of living and dying, and choice of an assisted death are in direct conflict with the beliefs and values of others.

This can be a significant problem when the opposing party is the patient's partner or an extremely close family member, especially if this person resides with the patient. Under such circumstances and under current laws, it would be foolhardy for you to agree to assist in the patient's death. You would risk indictment and prosecution, subsequent loss of your professional license, and perhaps a civil action for wrongful death brought by significant relations.

Opposition may be less of a problem when the patient lives alone or with a supportive partner and the opposing party is geographically removed or has been estranged from the patient for many years. This is not uncommon among patients with HIV disease and can also be seen when older adults are isolated from their adult children or other relatives. In such circumstances, it is not unusual, after years of separation, for a family member to reappear on the scene on hearing of the patient's condition and to be outraged when informed of the patient's plans to end his own life.

This potential conflict may be brought to your attention by the patient himself as a result of your questioning, or it may materialize in a call to your office from the concerned other. You may also be confronted by schism firsthand, when a patient requests your help in the presence of a significant relation and the latter immediately disagrees. This could occur in an exam room, a hospital setting, or the home of a patient under hospice care. Nurses and social workers within hospice systems frequently find themselves involved in such disagreements; for example, they may be pulled aside by a family member and informed of the patient's intentions.

The possibility of such situations arising makes it essential that you have a strategic response prepared in advance. What is also clear is that a patient must feel he can freely express his concerns to you without fear of confrontation or criticism by others.

You might decide to tell the patient to work out these conflicts on his own; you might suggest that the parties obtain professional counseling; or you might ignore the concerns altogether and help the patient die, even though you run the risk of subsequent pursuit by the opposing parties.

To ignore everyone's concerns denies them the importance they may deserve and fails to take into account the effects that the patient's assisted death may have on the people in his life. But if you decide to take the concerns of others into consideration, you have to further determine whether this will include both individuals who are close to the patient and those who are more distant. You might find yourself asking, "Should I worry about the opposition of a geographically distant parent of an adult man with AIDS?" or "Should I consider the opposition of an adult child of an older cancer patient who claims that he has been ignored by his children for years?"

In addressing such questions, you might try putting yourself in the positions of the parties involved. For example, would you want your opposition to count in a clinician's decision to assist in the death of your parent, your adult child, or some other relative? Do you think you should have any say in determining life and death matters for a person in your family? On the other hand, now assume the position of the patient. Do you believe your significant others should have the right to influence a decision on when and how you die? The answers you give to these questions should tell you something about your own ideas, values, and expectations of family and relationships.

If you decide to continue on to the next step, you clearly need more specific information about the interests of the opposing family member or significant relation. In particular, you need to know:

- What is the nature of the patient's relationship with this person?
- How was this person informed of the patient's decision, and why?
- What is the basis of this person's opposition?
- How might the patient's assisted death affect this other person?

In talking with the patient or the opposing other, you need to determine this person's importance in the life of the patient. You would do well to pay close attention to whether the patient includes this person in his concept of "family." If he does not, you need to learn why. For example, he may feel there is a clear distinction between a current significant relation and an estranged blood tie.

Next, you need to learn how this person was informed that the patient was considering the possibility of an assisted death. Was he told by yet another family member opposed to the patient's idea? Or was he directly informed by the patient, either in an attempt to discuss his plans and obtain support or in an effort to hurt this other party?

A thirty-five-year-old man suffering from AIDS told me in a discussion group how, in visiting his parents after years of separation, he found himself bringing up the topic of assisted suicide, and when the discussion "became heated," he told them he saw nothing wrong with it and was planning this for himself. The conflict escalated, and though he apologized to his mother, he cut his visit short before resolving matters with his father. He admitted that the visit had brought up a lot of old issues, and that his statements were probably a means of affirming his independence and also "irritating them a bit," given what he felt were their "intolerant social and religious beliefs." He added that he did not think their opposition would be a problem for him. He also did not rule out the possibility that they would pay him a surprise visit later on.

Your Role in the Face of Opposition

Potential opposition to a patient's decision can pose a serious problem for you as a health professional. If the patient has shared with significant relations his plan to seek your help, an agreement to assist might result in your being seen by opponents as an accomplice in his death. This could be especially troublesome if their opposition is rooted in deep beliefs, and if they have not had an opportunity to resolve their personal issues with the patient. If you follow through on your agreement, you could be held accountable for the patient's death and risk legal prosecution and sanctions from your licensing board. Although this has occurred in only a handful of cases over the past several years, the risk is something you must consider. In the event that serious opposition is expressed, you might

- Decline the patient's request
- Determine the nature of the opposition by discussing it in more detail with the patient
- Contact a hospice team member (if the patient is under hospice care) to learn more about any potential conflict in the patient's home

- Visit the patient at home to informally assess the problem, while maintaining confidentiality

- Suggest a meeting with the patient and the concerned party

The last approach would seem called for if this individual (1) is a partner or is otherwise important in the patient's life, (2) is involved in the practical care and emotional life of the patient, or (3) poses a serious potential risk to you as a health professional should you decide to help. Such a meeting can serve multiple purposes. It can help you

- Obtain insights into the relationship between this person and the patient

- Gain a clearer understanding of the patient's mental state and of any hidden factors that may be influencing his decision

- Correct faulty information this person may have about the patient's condition, prognosis, or possible treatment alternatives

- Obtain information from this person about her expectations regarding the patient's end-of-life care and the ethical, religious, or practical reasons for her opposition

In addition, such a meeting can help the two individuals communicate about a range of issues they may not yet have had the opportunity to discuss. Because both are likely to view this forum as important, they may express their thoughts more fully than they would under normal circumstances. The meeting can also serve the purpose of providing the participants with information about other available options and resources, such as hospice or respite for caregivers.

Before suggesting such a meeting, however, you must satisfy yourself that this represents an appropriate use of your time, given that the task could be performed at least as effectively by a skilled therapist or social worker. My own belief is that if you are willing to help a patient die, you should also be willing to personally explore whatever problems might stand in the way. Potential opposition is an obvious impediment to be looked at.

Further, it is vital that you articulate in advance the purpose of the consultation, as well as your own role in it. The patient must understand that your purpose is not to convince the other of the validity of his desire to end his life. Similarly, the opposing other needs to understand that the purpose is not to secure her permission to help the patient die—a consideration she may well have in mind if she sees you as the potential bearer of a lethal prescription. It must be made clear that the purpose of the meeting is to expand your awareness of each person's concerns and of other issues that may be affecting the patient's decision, and to provide the significant relation with whatever factual information you can offer about the patient's condition, the likely course of his illness, and his prognosis.

If you are a physician or nurse, remember that your task is not that of a therapist. You are not there to solve these individuals' interpersonal problems. Nor are you there to serve as a mediator or judge. You are simply meeting with these parties to learn the best way to deal with the patient's concerns. Nevertheless, know that each party is likely to have a different agenda, and both may be interested in convincing you of the validity of their opinion or in changing the position of the other. It is essential that you defuse the potential for conflict up front by setting firm boundaries and providing a clear purpose.

Although your intent is not to convince the opposing party of the reasonable nature of the patient's request, it is possible that she is in denial about the patient's actual condition or has a flawed understanding of his current health status, degree of suffering, and likely prognosis. With the patient's permission, it would be wise to begin by ensuring that the two parties share in the same basic knowledge. You might begin by asking the patient, "What have you told [the other] about your condition? What have you shared with her about what you have been going through?" You could then ask the other party what she has been told and what she understands. You might ask her if there is anything about the patient's condition or home life of which you should be aware. Such a question opens the way for her to voice her concerns about the patient's plans for an assisted death.

It is crucial that you refuse to get drawn into an argumentative dialogue. You must also avoid being put on the defensive. After all, you have not yet agreed to help the patient die, and you are meeting simply to talk about the patient's condition and treatment options, to provide information, and to discuss any concerns either party may have. If necessary, these points should be reiterated.

COERCION AND OTHER INFLUENCES

Any alleged support of a patient's decision by significant relations needs to be assessed for the potential presence of coercion. Forcible influence may come from family members, other significant relations, or from the patient himself. The main questions you need to answer are

- How much of the patient's decision to seek aid in dying is of her own desire?

- Has the patient been influenced by anyone in asking for your help?

- Has the patient coerced others into providing their support for this decision?

Coercion by Others

Opponents of assisted suicide often argue that if the practice is legalized, it would lend itself to the coercion of vulnerable patients by unscrupulous family members. In talking with hundreds of terminal and incurably ill patients over the past several years, I have yet to hear this complaint directly voiced. Nevertheless, I am certain that coercion does occur in varying forms and degrees. It may be present, too, in other end-of-life decisions, such as the withholding or withdrawal of treatment, and even in the writing and use of advance directives. The looser the definition of *coercion* that is applied, the more instances one could identify, including some where there was no intent to coerce.

What I term "coercion" of a patient by others can take several forms. It does not have to consist of family members or other relations strongly recommending an assisted death. In its most hidden and innocent form, coercion takes place when family members or significant others, exhausted from the daily burden of caregiving, begin to withdraw from the patient or convey subtle signs of irritability. This can initiate a downward spiral that eventually leads to the patient seeing assisted death as "a way out" or a means of alleviating the stress of her illness on others. The spiral continues when the patient speaks of this option and weary caregivers embrace it. She may have voiced such thoughts only to let others know the depth of her despair or to receive validation that her life still has value. When the idea is endorsed, she is likely to hear the opposite message—that she is, indeed, "in the way."

A woman who raised the possibility of assisted suicide in the face of an imminent move to a convalescent facility told me of her despair on hearing her daughter agree with her:

I admit I didn't know what I wanted, and was feeling sorry for myself, and maybe she went along to shock me out of it, but I still feel hurt. Now I don't know what I want anymore.

Although she had been a longtime supporter of the "right to die," the lack of positive emotional support from her daughter, her feelings of isolation, and the severe limitations on her range of choices sapped her will and left her feeling unable to pursue any course of action. "I guess what I really want," she said, "is to feel that someone cares for me, and I don't feel this right now."

In this case, as in many others, the caregiver's intention in accepting the patient's proposal was to provide support. As the woman's daughter told me, "She talked about it so much, over the years and recently, I thought this was what she wanted." Nevertheless, her failure to verbally express her love for her mother—which resulted partly from her guilt over the lack of options for her mother's care—sent the wrong signal. An open dialogue about these concerns eventually proved to be the key and brought the two women together.

Some significant relations readily agree with a patient's request in order to avoid feeling the full measure of their own despair and their anguish at being unable to help the patient live a fuller and more enjoyable life. They may be unable to accept the approaching death of their loved one, and like some patients, may prefer to escape rather than face their feelings or talk about them. Unfortunately, this inability to talk openly about issues can drive a patient and her family toward a decision that no one fully desires.

At a later stage, coercion of a different form may come about. Exhausted family members and others, having agreed with a patient's desire to die, may begin to feel a certain frustration if the assisted death is long in coming. During the course of a terminal illness, especially following the prognosis of death, a psychological adjustment often takes place that allows the family and other significant relations to accept the inevitable end. This enables them to gradually shift their orientation from one of hope to one of preparation for the person's death. Once this shift occurs, however, the protracted dying process and the demands of constant care can weigh heavily on those surrounding the patient. Before long, they desire to get back to life as it was or to start their lives over. If the patient has declared her intention to die with assistance, they may put subtle—or not so subtle—pressure on her to carry this plan through.

A few of my interviewees admitted to urging a patient to pursue the agreed-on plan. Two of them had shifted from initial opposition to acceptance of assisted death. Each later began worrying that the patient—in one case, a father with cancer, in the other, a brother with multiple sclerosis—was taking too long to initiate it. They were concerned that the patient would soon lose his ability to speak or swallow, and therefore would become incapable of asking for or ingesting a lethal medication.

The daughter of the cancer patient told me that had her father waited any longer to ask his doctor for help, he would have been unable to do so. She knew that the result would have been his pressuring her to secure the drugs on her own, something she did not desire to do. She said she repeatedly asked him, "If you're ever going to do this, isn't it time you talked to your doctor?" Eventually he did, and was successful in obtaining the medications that ended his life several weeks later.

In the other case, the patient's sister, a nurse practitioner, finally supplied him with the lethal drug he had been requesting for years. Months then went by, and he seemed to be losing his ability to swallow. She began to worry that "if he didn't take it soon, he would lose his window of opportunity." A related worry was that she would eventually be forced to give him a lethal injection. This was something she had no interest in doing. She said, "I was getting angry. I kept telling him that I would not get any more involved, and that time was running out." As a result of her demands, he finally carried out his plan.

In both these instances, it is safe to say that the patients followed through only because they were urged to do so by others. Without such prompting, it is anyone's guess what the eventual outcome would have been. The nurse practitioner expressed her regret that her prompting had resulted in his death—a death for which he may have been emotionally unprepared. "I was angry, exhausted, and worried," she said, "and all of this took its toll on me."

Adding to the possibility of coercion by others is the diminished sense of self-worth that may be experienced by a patient during a life-altering illness. Together with a feeling of no longer being important to relatives and friends, this can lead the patient to believe that her own needs are secondary to those of others or that she has become a burden to them, both practically and financially. Such an outlook can set up the patient for coercion, or at least color how she interprets the situation within her household. She may, for example, blame herself for any economic difficulties her significant others are experiencing, whether or not there is any evidence that she is the cause. She may similarly see herself as the culprit in any relationship problems around her.

When patients develop such an inflated notion of their influence on the lives of others—the amazing power they hold by virtue of their illness—it is no surprise that some see death as the optimal solution. Although they can be said to have coerced themselves into this position, significant others have been accomplices by virtue of their withdrawal or their inability to communicate their true feelings to the patient. The expression of feelings is not always easy, of course, especially given the daily toil of caregiving and lack of opportunity to talk, a belief that grief must be repressed, the emotional numbness that often masks deep pain, and a tradition of reticence around matters of the heart.

Coercion by Patients

Patients, too, can be a source of coercion. It is not unusual for patients—especially those used to being the center of control within their households—to attempt to sway or manipulate others into agreeing with their decision. This can be a source of great stress for significant others, especially if they have not had adequate time or opportunity to achieve a sense of closure in their relationship with the patient. Such coercion might also create a problem for you, as a clinician, if you agree to participate in this person's death. It is possible, for example, that those who have been coerced will transfer their guilt and feelings of responsibility to you, attempting to hold you accountable. The legal and professional effects of this could be enormous.

A patient who is suffering can wield a great deal of power, even to the point of quieting potential dissent on the decision to die. This power, drawing on the stark realities of illness and potential death, can entrance others. It acquires even greater force from the guilt of family members and significant relations about their perceived failings with respect to the patient and from the grief they are already experiencing.

Also contributing to the responsiveness of others to the patient's insistence on assisted death is the burden of caregiving itself, the strain of responding to the patient's continual demands, and the difficulty of tending to someone who may be suffering intolerably. The caregiver may simply give in and agree with the patient's decision, even against his own best interests and moral beliefs. The subtle message "My rights are of more immediate concern" or "Your needs don't matter—I'm the one who's dying" can be emotionally compelling. One man told me about his wife's anger at his hesitation over helping her die. "You're part of this relationship," she railed, "and this is what I need. Next month you'll still have a life. I won't!"

Family agreement can also be accentuated by the private relationship that caregiving often entails and by the illegal status of assisted suicide. Without opportunities to discuss the issue openly with others, excessive secrecy can lead to a sense of isolation and of limited options.

Questions to Ask Yourself

Although your patient is your primary responsibility, it is crucial that you understand him in relation to others. It is also essential that you have some awareness of the concerns of the significant people in his life, especially if you make the decision to help him die. Ignoring their needs can prove to be detrimental to everyone involved, including you.

Unlike a natural death, which speaks for itself and cannot be argued against, an assisted death is different. Because of its premature nature, it creates the potential for contentiousness and finger-pointing. It allows dissatisfied others to transfer to you any responsibility they may feel for having failed the patient.

An assisted death is not merely a medical procedure; it is inherently a social act. As such, it requires a full understanding of the social world of which the patient is a part. This means taking into account the human factors that may be influencing his decision, as well as what his act might mean for those who, by virtue of their relationship with him, are participants in his death and its consequences.

You will be required, at times, to step out of your role as a health professional and take on both investigative and pastoral duties. You will be looking at relationships and patterns of communication—not only the very private communication that takes place between you and your patient but also communication between the patient and others, and sometimes between these others and you. And much of the information you need will be obtained by probing for it. This work is indispensable, for in deciding to assist in a patient's death, you are stepping on sacred ground—that of family and relationship.

To reduce the potential negative effects of assisting in a death, you might ask yourself the following questions:

- Have the patient and his significant relations been provided with adequate information on all other options? Do I have further information on alternatives that I might provide? Have the patient and those around him taken the time to fully consider alternatives? If not, how do I intend to respond?

- Do I have an adequate understanding of the patient's home life, family, and relationships? If not, do I know how I might gather such information?

- Do there appear to be any underlying family issues or conflicts that might be motivating the patient? Are there obvious communication problems between him and others that might be affecting his decision?

- Have I seen any evidence of serious conflicts between the patient's values and his decision to seek my help in dying? Have I discussed this apparent conflict with him?

- Has the patient informed those closest to him of his intentions? If not, do I believe that his reasons for secrecy are valid? If I do not, how do I intend to respond?

- If the patient has informed others of his intentions, do they support his decision? Am I certain he has not pressured them into supporting his decision? Have I asked them? Have they considered the effects of this action on themselves?

- Am I certain the patient is not being influenced in his decision by others? Am I certain he is making the decision as a free choice? If not, what further steps do I need to take?

- Am I certain that no significant relations oppose the patient's decision? If not, how might I gain this information? If others are opposed, do I understand their reasons?

- Has the patient provided significant others any opportunities to resolve interpersonal issues and achieve closure? From what I know, have these opportunities been adequate? If not, am I still comfortable with the patient's reasons for requesting my help?

- Has the patient thoroughly considered the consequences for others of his planned action? Has he recognized who might be affected and how? Has he considered the effects on a range of others who may initially be unaware of the cause of his death but may learn of it later? If not, am I comfortable with this?

- Will the nature of this death create ethical or moral difficulties for family members or significant others who know of his plans but oppose the decision? Am I comfortable with this?

- Have I thoroughly considered the consequences, for others and for myself, of helping this patient die? Have I weighed the professional risks against potential opposition from others?

***

Historically, clinicians were usually concerned with entire families. The illness of one person affected all, and the decisions of the family took precedence over the leanings of any one member. Actions were taken for the good of the family and the patient. Moreover, clinicians addressed themselves not only to the patient's physical well-being but also to his general welfare as a person.

Changes in medical practice, family life, and law have transformed the clinician's role. No longer does the primary care provider necessarily treat the whole family unit. The individual patient has become the focus, and her autonomy has become paramount. Outside of hospice and smaller communities, clinicians are not even necessarily aware of the most important features of a patient's daily life. A family medical history in a patient's file no longer brings to mind the faces of others. They are unknown. It is highly unlikely that a patient, her partner, family members, and other significant relations all see the same clinician. Instead, as David Loxterkamp has stated:

> More and more of us have moved under the shelter of the corporation [managed care], passing patients between specialty pools of preferred providers, to control "risk" through the use of practice guidelines, and to pursue only those clinical questions that can be answered expeditiously. We are specialists. We have a job to do, one that is limited by the clock, the protocol, and our role at the bedside, which we have increasingly consigned to mid-level technicians.

The situation that Loxterkamp describes is real and increasingly inescapable. But in considering the question of whether or not to help a patient die, you must attempt to step outside of such constraints and practice a very different form of medicine. Your questions need to be more than clinical, because this is more than a clinical decision. It is one that goes to the very soul of the patient—and to the very soul of clinical practice. Further, as the patient's living and dying are both apt to involve others—partners and family members—it is a decision that must take the existence and interests of these others into account. This is no small challenge.

What I am suggesting is that a patient's suffering and personal autonomy may not always give you sufficient grounds for comfort with his decision, particularly given the illegality of the act. However, I am not saying that family opinion must take precedence. Your primary responsibility is to the patient. The course I am advising is to expand the range of factors you consider when weighing a decision. If you do not, you may find yourself walking on dangerous ground.

By now, you should have a fairly clear conception of the knowledge that is required if you are to make a responsible and humane decision. You must be aware of your patient's innermost motivations for seeking your help, her physical condition and her experience with illness, the situation within her home, her relationships with others, and any other outside factors that may be affecting her desire to end her life. It is also important that you have a fairly good understanding of the positions of significant others and their own motives in supporting or opposing the patient's plan.

In the next chapter, we will put all this information together, and we will also switch gears, turning our attention to you and to your final decision to help.

5

Working Through the Choices

Helping a patient die is not solely a medical act or a response to physiological facts and suffering. It is also an inherently social act, one that should be performed only after considering the emotions and spirit, as well as the body and personal relationships, of the patient.

This broader appeal has seldom been a primary consideration within medicine. Psychosocial issues are usually passed off to others. Although medical professionals may well be the first to assess such problems, they often see them as interfering with the expeditious practice of medicine. The emotional life of the patient therefore becomes the domain of the psychiatrist, psychotherapist, or counselor. Similarly, troubles of the spirit, if not deemed psychiatric, are shifted to pastoral counselors, priests, rabbis, or ministers.

The patient's request for your help in dying changes all of this. As a health care professional, you are now the first line of defense, the most powerful guard at the gate between life and death. This is an awesome responsibility and challenge. But it carries a potential for great good, for healing in broader dimensions.

Achievement of this potential, however, requires that you bear in mind the patient's full range of concerns throughout the processes of caring for her and deciding whether or not to help her die. As I will show, these two activities should be intimately woven together, with the emphasis placed on comfort care. Your decision to help this person die should not be separate from your caring role. Rather, it should arise out of quality treatment and palliative care, which may ultimately make the decision to assist irrelevant. After all, care based on compassionate concern is frequently perceived by patients as the component that is most lacking in their health care experience. When it is provided, the fear of an intolerable future with worsening pain and suffering, the sense of isolation and abandonment, often dissolve—along with the desire to bring life to an end.

A CARE-BASED GUIDE TO DECISION MAKING

On receiving a patient's request for a hastened death, you are confronted with the opportunity to respond to the full range of the patient's needs. Certainly this includes deciding whether or not to assist. Beyond that, however, you are faced with how best to respond in terms of treatment and referral decisions that ensure quality care. These two elements go hand in hand, as the decision to aid in a patient's death is dependent on fully understanding and responding to all of her concerns.

To help illuminate these processes, I have designed a decision tree (Figure 5.1) to guide you through the various aspects of the decision process. Regardless of whether you ever decide to help your patient die, the steps I enumerate will aid you in working with her clinically. If you do decide to assist, your understanding of this decision process can help reduce your risk of being legally challenged for wrongful actions. And with this analytical tool at your disposal, you will be less inclined to feel that there are only two possible responses to a request, outright rejection and immediate agreement.

There is more to this decision than merely assessing a patient's condition and then either agreeing or refusing to help. As you can see from Figure 5.1, the request for your help should trigger a range of personal and clinical decisions. The first is an immediate assessment of your ethical concerns. You may say to yourself, "I could

FIGURE 5.1 Assisted Suicide Decision Tree.

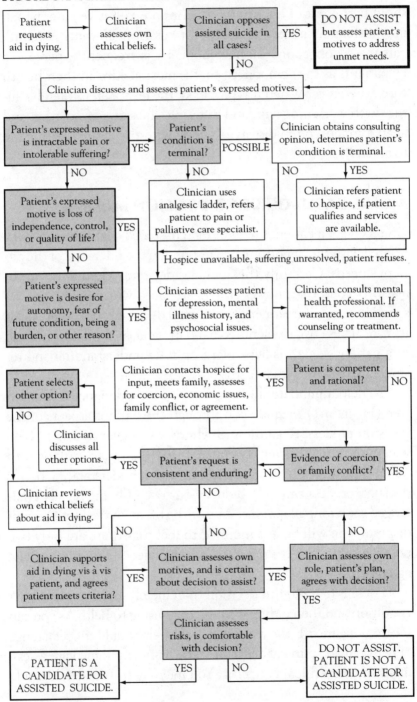

never help a patient die" or "I don't know what I might do. I need to consider this further before I decide."

Regardless of your initial ethical response, you are under an obligation to clearly assess your patient's motives, obtaining as much information as you can to make the best treatment decisions possible. In the decision tree, the arrows lead from a few of the commonly expressed motives to actions you might consider taking. I have discussed these potential responses in detail in the preceding chapters. For example, the patient's claim of intractable pain or intolerable suffering should be met immediately with appropriate treatment and referrals. Evaluating your patient for potential depression or prior mental health problems is also critical, and this would be followed, if necessary, by referrals for counseling, treatment, or a full mental health assessment.

If you are a physician or nursing professional, you will obviously be aware of the clinical actions that are indicated when various motives are expressed. You may also be quite knowledgeable about other resources in your local area that can effectively address the health-related needs of the patient. Beyond this, depending on your particular training and experience, you may be moving into less clearly charted territory. For example, you may feel relatively ill-equipped to assess for hidden psychosocial issues or to look for evidence of family pressures, conflicts, or coercion. In such cases, I suggest referring back to the previous chapters for some ideas on how to proceed.

If you are a mental health professional, I recommend reviewing Figure 5.1 to obtain a better understanding of the broad range of issues that might be relevant in working with your client. Knowing this person's motives and fears, and the medical approaches he has accepted or rejected to date, will help you to delve into other areas of his experience and perhaps to understand, even question, the quality of care he has received so far.

To begin this process, review the decision tree as you look over the following list of patient-related actions and tasks that must precede any final decision:

- Make sure that you and your patient understand one another, regardless of any possible differences in cultural background, ethnicity, or language.

- Conduct a preliminary review of your ethical beliefs concerning assisted dying, using Chapter One as a guide.

- Clearly tell your patient, if you are morally opposed to assisted dying or cannot justify your involvement, that you cannot help him.

- Continue to consider the request if you are comfortable so far, but do not make any specific promises.

- Inform your patient that you intend to work with him closely, will address all of his concerns, and will aggressively respond to them, regardless of your ethical position and your willingness to consider assisting in his death.

- Listen closely to the motives the patient has expressed for seeking your assistance and (with the help of Chapters Two and Three) assess the request for possible hidden or unexpressed motivations.

- Discuss all issues and (again referring to Chapter Three) attempt to separate current physiological complaints from fear of future conditions.

- Obtain all the facts about your patient's physical condition and prognosis, seeking a consulting opinion or further diagnostic procedures if necessary.

- If intractable pain is involved, assess your own skills in pain control and treat the patient aggressively, using a treatment approach such as that described by Kathleen Foley in her 1985 article and Gary Johanson in his 1984 handbook or the "analgesic ladder" depicted by Vittorio Ventafridda and detailed by the World Health Organization (WHO).

- Refer your patient to a physician experienced in palliative care or pain control if the patient is not terminal and you do not feel qualified to treat his pain and suffering.

- Refer your patient to hospice if he is terminal, emphasizing to him the benefits of this course. Be willing to make this referral early, before the patient's suffering intensifies.

- Discuss more deeply with your patient such issues as quality of life, loss of autonomy, independence, and dignity, as well as economic and health insurance concerns and any perception he may have of burdening others.

- Listen closely for the presence of contradictory values, as revealed in the patient's lifestyle, relationship patterns, religious beliefs, and reasons for wanting to die.

- Assess your patient for possible depression or mental illness by reviewing his comments and medical history. (See techniques described in Chapter Three.)

- Consult a mental health professional for evaluation; assessment of rationality, competence, and impulsivity; and possible treatment of depression.

- Recommend that your patient seek psychological or pastoral counseling if you believe he might benefit.

- Determine the presence of any psychosocial issues, family pressures, or interpersonal conflict, using the process and questions described in Chapter Four.

- Contact the hospice team—if he is a hospice patient—for insights into his home life and potential conflicts.

- Recommend that he and significant relations seek counseling for any apparent interpersonal problems and offer to meet with him and any closely involved parties to discuss his condition and treatment.

- Assess the nature of support for the patient's decision from his partner or significant relations and look for the presence of subtle coercion of the patient by the family—or vice versa.

- Confirm the consistent and enduring nature of the patient's request. (This will be discussed in Chapter Six.)

- Discuss all available treatment options with the patient and his significant other. (I will describe a few of these later in this chapter.)

THOUGHTS ABOUT COMMUNICATION

It should be clear from the list we have just examined that quality communication is the key component throughout. It begins with the patient's request and expression of motives. Your understanding of that request, and your ability to assess possible underlying motives for it, depend on your willingness to engage the patient in dialogue and on the skills you bring to that dialogue.

Your patient's request may itself result from an inability to communicate her concerns to you. She may be hesitant to discuss certain issues, to ask necessary questions, or to make clear her very real complaints and fears. Because of her failure to discuss all her issues openly and receive feedback, she may come to assume that no options exist except assisted dying, or that her suffering is indeed irreversible. Moreover, she may misinterpret your busy office schedule and less than relaxed manner as disinterest or abandonment. Long before this, her fears about being in the way, or burdening others—family members, caregivers, *and* clinicians—may have been silently suppressed, leading her to decide that assisted death was her only answer.

On hearing a patient ask for your help, your most appropriate response is to immediately reassess the quality of the communication you have had with this person. You would do well to see this request, first and foremost, as a plea to talk fully about the broad range of issues that are driving the patient's decision. Thus the request for help can serve as an opportunity not just to talk about this option but to alter the very nature of the clinician-patient relationship.

This is the intent behind the list just presented. It is not solely a checklist to aid in your decision making. It is also a list of actions and tasks that can add richness to this relationship, helping you to form a deeper human bond, regardless of whether you personally can ever support the patient's request.

The list requires a commitment of time and action, and I fully understand the professional and practical constraints on the course I am recommending. This type of discussion and action may not seem practical in the current environment of managed care. I therefore offer these recommendations for use by a health care team. I also offer them to the individual clinician as an ideal, knowing full well that not all of the steps I have enumerated may be accomplished. Nevertheless, they should be attempted. The act of agreeing to help a patient die is so serious that it demands attention to many, if not most, of the listed concerns. A decision to hasten a patient's death should never be made in a moment, for informed consent is not enough. Great thought is demanded—far more than is required for any treatment decision—for the act in question is not solely medical but both social and final.

This extraordinary situation calls for more than technical skills, although these, too, are critical. A patient's request and your response to it elevate the importance of the human and interpersonal dimensions of care.

During these rare times, medicine has to become an art, dependent not only on diagnostic and treatment skills and knowledge of options but also on the clinician's intuitive and creative faculties, on her ability to use words both to explore and to reassure.

This human component thrives best when communication is not blunted, and when both patients and clinicians feel at ease in each other's presence. In such conditions, medicine can be practiced at its deepest level, rooted in mutual trust and compassion. The patient does not hesitate to share her innermost concerns, and the clinician feels free to mine the depths of the patient's fears and desires for the sake of a therapeutic understanding. At this level, it can be said that medicine is indeed an art.

The same can be said of mental health professionals. Clients with terminal or life-altering conditions need to be able to talk safely and openly about their desires without facing the unnecessary risk of intervention or involuntary hospitalization, particularly if they are competent and rational. Instead of immediately labeling talk on the topic as depressive suicidal ideation, you would do well to hear such statements as invitations to explore the full range of thoughts and emotions that surround the issue. The discussion that ensues may result in vast improvements in a client's relationships, outlook on living and dying, and overall quality of life.

The performance of medicine can only be enhanced when a sanctuary exists for the free communication of concerns. Conversely, anything that might stand in the way of such communication can adversely affect the quality of care. In the circumstances we are discussing, detachment—often a protection for both patients and professionals—will not work. Instead, I recommend that you

- Express your willingness to talk openly with your patient about all of her concerns
- Attempt to discuss all issues clearly, and in terminology understandable to the patient
- Answer every question from the patient as honestly as possible
- Be emotionally supportive and nonjudgmental, regardless of your stance toward assisted suicide
- Let your patient know that you understand the importance of fully exploring every issue, but that many emotional concerns are best dealt with in a relationship with a therapist

PAIN AND SUFFERING REVISITED

Another key factor that can be seen throughout the decision tree is the status of the patient's physical condition. The primary issues here are whether his condition is terminal or incurable and whether he is experiencing intractable pain or suffering intolerably from symptoms or loss of function. By now, open discussion has revealed the extent of the patient's dissatisfaction with his medical treatment and the direction of his illness.

The central issue could be inadequate pain relief, side effects from pain-relieving medications, or fear of future intolerable pain—based on the patient's current or prior experiences. If some of these concerns can potentially be resolved with little effort and minimal invasive procedures, I cannot stress enough the need to attempt this prior to your agreeing to help in the patient's death.

As the earlier list recommends, begin by offering the patient—without hesitation or restriction—the highest-quality pain control required to elevate his pain threshold. Treat the patient aggressively, using an approach such as the "analgesic ladder." This begins with the use of nonopioids, such as aspirin or ibuprofen or other NSAIDs, and gradually moves up to weak, intermediate, and finally, strong opioids. In addition, if you have not done so,

- Pay close attention to psychological, emotional, and social factors that may intensify stress, anxiety, and the overall experience of pain, and urge the patient to seek counseling or spiritual support for these concerns

- Respond to problems of insomnia that can intensify the pain experience

- Attend to the pathologic processes that can lead to pain, using appropriate treatments—if accepted by the patient—ranging from antibiotics and radiation to hormone therapy, surgery, or other drugs or procedures as indicated by the specific condition

- Consider other pain treatment approaches, including co-analgesics, the interruption of the pathways of pain, or non-drug measures like physical therapy, acupuncture, and massage

There is no reason for taking a conservative approach to pain control. This is especially true if your patient has a terminal condition or if he might otherwise choose death to avoid unnecessary suffering.

In most circumstances, a referral to hospice should be your first line of defense. If the prognosis and conditions are right, home palliative care can be particularly valuable for treating a range of symptoms, especially physical pain. A patient seeking your help may reject this idea, out of emotional exhaustion or for some other reason, but it is vital to emphasize its benefits. You might even make such a referral a condition of your continuing to consider the patient's request. If he continues to reject the idea of further treatment or palliative care, you will obviously need to think deeply before agreeing to assist in his death.

Part of the reason for such a refusal may well be the patient's overall experience with pain and suffering, and the deterioration in his quality of life. Another part may be related to his emotional suffering, his exhausting career as a patient, and his desire to end both the physical and the emotional torment of a terminal or incurable condition.

If you are a physician or nursing professional, there is little you can do directly to resolve the issue of emotional pain, other than continuing to provide the best all-around care. The latter would include palliative, emotional, and even pastoral support, and referral of the patient to a compassionate mental health professional for counseling or treatment. Remember, however, that emotional pain is not always the same thing as depression. It can have far deeper dimensions and does not always lend itself to traditional psychiatric treatment or psychological interventions. Some of its elements may be better treated with spiritual or pastoral counseling. Here again, look into the possibility of hospice care, with its emphasis on psychospiritual support.

If you are a mental health professional, you should remember these same points. You should know also that the opportunity for a patient to talk with you openly about the full range of his concerns can do much to reduce the emotional exhaustion and anxiety that intensify physical pain and suffering. In addition, you can serve as a compassionate source of practical advice, even convincing the patient, when appropriate, of the benefits both of mood-elevating medications and of palliative care.

The Problem of Undermedication

Patients may be resistant to further attempts to deal with their physical pain because of their current or prior experience of being undermedicated. They may also have encountered serious side effects from previous pain medications. This type of history, which may have undermined the patient's trust in the helping professions, is often difficult to overcome. The problem reflects the continuing emphasis in medicine on cure as opposed to care, and it highlights the critical need for further clinical education in palliative care and pain relief.

Undertreatment of pain is a serious issue. According to hospice staff with whom I have talked, it is a particular problem among primary care physicians and certain specialists—including many oncologists—who often refuse to define a patient as terminally ill until it is obvious to all that this person is dying.

Some health professionals feel that providing patients with strong pain medication is unprofessional in that it focuses on treating symptoms rather than causes. There are those who seem to believe that pain and suffering are a small price to pay for the opportunity to achieve a cure, even when all signs point to the patient's impending death. Others have been taught that the use of strong pain medication, such as morphine, to make a patient comfortable diminishes professional control and in some instances interferes with optimal patient care by masking symptoms. As a result, they may not want to provide morphine except as a last resort.

Hospice personnel and pain management specialists with whom I have spoken have also pointed to societal attitudes, and the culture of medicine itself, as sources of this problem. In particular:

- Effective pain-relieving medications are strongly regulated, and many clinicians do not want to prescribe them because they fear disciplinary action by government agencies and medical boards.

- Doctors' attitudes to pain medications reflect their education on the subject, which is typically poor, as well as societal opposition to narcotics and other drugs that change people's sensorium or that can be used for recreational purposes.

- Physicians sometimes feel that using strong pain control and referring a patient to hospice are signs of giving up, even when these approaches can clearly be supportive and help with a patient's treatment and comfort.

In addition, clinicians are trained to regard strong pain medication as dangerous. The common view is that opioids have serious side effects that are difficult to manage. These include addiction and decreased respiration that may lead to death. In rebuttal, Ira Byock has stated, in a 1993 article:

> While . . . tolerance to narcotic medication can occur, it is never a significant problem in palliative care practice. During the course of a progressive illness like cancer, it is common for people to require intermittent increases in their dose of narcotic pain medication. Whether the required increase is due to tolerance, progression of the disease, or a combination of the two is usually a moot question. In any case, increasing the dose . . . usually suffices. There is no maximum dose above which it is impossible to go. The right dose is the dose that works.

Although this is reassuring, the amount of medication that is sometimes necessary to alleviate serious pain can result in other side effects that are considered "intolerable" by the patient. Although many side effects, such as drowsiness, may diminish or be eliminated over time, there are patients for whom clarity of thought and total alertness are synonymous with an acceptable quality of life. Keep this in mind, as it may be an important factor in your decision.

Bringing Others In

Throughout this discussion, I have called attention to the need to seek the opinions and guidance of other professionals. This protects both you and the patient. For example, I have pointed to the wisdom of seeking a consulting opinion from a specialist whose skills and opinions you trust. Such a consultation will be crucial if you are not yourself a specialist in the area of the patient's illness, if you are unfamiliar with all the aspects of this condition, if the patient has a chronic, irreversible, or degenerative condition, or if the illness often has a questionable prognosis.

I have also strongly emphasized the value of referring your patient to a psychiatrist, psychologist, or other psychotherapist for counseling or for assessment of competency, rationality, voluntariness, impulsivity, and possible depression. A compassionate therapist who is experienced in working with terminal or incurable patients may be particularly skilled in identifying and treating depression, as may be a psychiatrist with geriatric experience. Such treatment must be administered gently, with due regard to possible drug sensitivities, the often fragile nature of a terminal patient's system, and the wide range of physiological symptoms already being experienced.

I have similarly argued the benefits of hospice, which offers both high-quality care and possible in-depth assessment of the patient's psychosocial situation. Contact with members of the hospice team can give you valuable insights into the patient's current condition, into significant physical, psychological, or environmental changes, into difficulties or stressors within the home, and into other psychosocial issues that might be pertinent to the patient's decision to die and to your own response.

In arguing for the inclusion of others in this process, I am not suggesting any violation of clinician-patient confidentiality. That can be maintained even as you consult with informed professionals or significant relations on the patient's physical condition, mental health status, and home situation.

However, there may be circumstances in which your need for professional support does require you to breach confidentiality. It can be extremely helpful, for example, to discuss with a trusted clinician the general features of the case and your own thoughts or reservations about helping this patient die. Or if you are a member of a hospital ethics committee, you might want to present the case for comments and advice. Confidentiality is preserved by focusing on the specifics of the case while withholding identifiable features.

The current legal status of assisted suicide makes many clinicians fearful of discussing it. They believe cases must be kept under wraps to protect everyone involved. True protection would reside in the ability to discuss such cases and to follow established clinical care guidelines, but this is currently not possible. Meanwhile, the privacy of the clinician-patient relationship is intensified by the questionable legal and ethical nature of the act. Hemmed in by the constraints on open discussion, the clinician may develop a form of tunnel vision. Exposure to the ideas of others can expand her perspective and increase her knowledge of other options.

HASTENING DEATH

Assisted suicide is not the only means of hastening death. The same result can be achieved by using high-dose morphine to depress respiration (the "double effect"), by removing life-sustaining treatment, by voluntary cessation of food and water consumption, and by sedating the patient to coma. Such options may be far more acceptable to a patient's partner or family members if these individuals are opposed to assisted death. There is also the option of euthanasia—the direct administration of a lethal substance to cause immediate death—which, like assisted suicide, is illegal. Each needs to be covered briefly.

Double Effect

Double effect requires a constantly administered dose of morphine, often via a morphine "pump." Although deaths are frequently hastened in this manner, ethically they must be approached in the same way as euthanasia, as they typically require dosages far beyond those needed to control pain. Depending on the patient's established tolerance for morphine, such dosages may be difficult or impossible to justify on the patient's drug chart. Moreover, this approach usually requires the involvement of a nursing professional, who controls the drug delivery device and titrates or otherwise alters the dosage on the orders of the patient's physician. This adds yet another ethical component to be considered.

Removal of Life-Sustaining Treatment

If the patient is receiving some form of life-sustaining treatment, the removal of such treatment can usually accelerate the process of natural death. This can be easily pictured in the case of a fully conscious patient with severe emphysema who is breathing with the help of a ventilator and wants to die. The removal of such treatment (as well as the withdrawal of artificial nutrition and hydration) by the patient's direct request, advance directive, or proxy has been legal in nearly every state since *Cruzan*. After the patient is taken off the respirator, he can be given a sedative medication that will relax him to the point where he is not suffering. In situations of this kind, it is apparent that assisted death is unnecessary.

Cessation of Food and Water

Another approach is for the patient to request the end of tube feeding or attempt to voluntarily cease consumption of food and water. Depending on the patient, her ability to swallow, and her closeness to death, this may require great willpower at first. Hospice personnel frequently claim that the sensation of hunger usually disappears in a day or two and that patients typically experience mild euphoria. Nevertheless, by withholding nutrition, it may take several days or even weeks for the patient to die. Many palliative care specialists argue that it then makes no sense to continue providing the patient with fluids by IV. Withholding fluids results in a buildup of toxins, which cause a natural anesthetic reaction, euphoria, and kidney failure—usually within a few days. For a patient with advanced cancer, AIDS, heart disease, or one of many other terminal conditions, death by dehydration may be a viable option. With proper sedation, the dying process can be relatively gentle.

This may work well for patients with end-stage disease, who often naturally lose the sensation of hunger or thirst. The major problem, however, is often with the patient's significant others. As one clinician told me, food struggles with families are quite common. If you and your patient decide on this option, your task—or that of hospice personnel—will be to educate the patient's family about the nature of this experience and the likely lack of suffering on the part of the patient.

When death is not imminent, the decision is more difficult for all involved. But this option may be the only practicable one when a patient wants to die and significant relations do not support the option of an assisted death.

Sedation to Coma

A related approach, used especially when a patient is in extreme pain and near death, is what has been called "terminal sedation" or "sedation to coma." Typically, patients are injected with a benzodiazepine such as Versed or Valium or a barbiturate such as thiopental, either of which will induce pharmacologic coma. In most instances, the patient is given neither nutrition nor water; if fluids are given, the IV fluid rate is substantially reduced. At first, the patient is lightly sedated and even able to talk, but he soon falls into what has been termed euphemistically a "twilight sleep." Unable to eat or drink, he usually dies as a result of kidney failure due to depletion of fluids or from pneumonia or heart attack.

This technique is used particularly for hospice patients close to death. In fact, as reported by Ronald Dworkin, one brief to the U.S. Supreme Court has stated that between 5 percent and 52 percent of dying patients entering home palliative care programs are terminally sedated. This approach can also be used in hospital settings.

Terminal Sedation Versus Assisted Dying

Hospice programs differ in terms of their philosophy on sedation. For some, the patient must be very close to death and either unconscious or suffering from intolerable pain that cannot be relieved in any other way. In other programs, however, such criteria are not specified. As one hospice physician told me:

> We do frequently sedate patients to coma. That's when it's called for by the symptoms and the process of dying itself. But you have to distinguish that from the patient who is alert, not at all agitated or delirious, and saying, "Hey, I want to end it all." That's much more of a judgment call, and you have to go with your feelings and opinions.

As in the case of death caused by depression of respiration following massive doses of morphine, death during terminal sedation can be seen as a secondary effect, for the initial purpose of sedation is to ease discomfort. Nevertheless, as one palliative care physician told me:

> Let's be honest: comfort is not the only goal. If it were, doctors would keep the IV fluid rate high, but in most instances they don't. If you pick a slow rate, the patient dies. Obviously, death is another goal. The real sign of intent is how you feel every morning when you're told the patient is still alive, and how you feel when they finally die. Are you overjoyed they're still alive? You're saddened when they die, but are you disappointed?

Although supporters of sedation to coma, like Ira Byock, claim that it is substantially different from euthanasia, others disagree. Proponents of assisted dying claim that this approach lacks honesty and that the only differences between it and euthanasia are in timing and personnel: death can take several days, and the medication is provided by nurses, not doctors. There are some in the hospice movement who agree with this judgment, calling sedation to coma "slow euthanasia." Interestingly, this is not a criticism but an acknowledgment that the approach is an important tool to ensure comfort when nothing else is available.

However you may view this practice, there can be a substantial psychological difference between terminal sedation and assisted dying, both for clinicians and for surviving family members. And this difference holds for assisted suicide as well as euthanasia. On the positive side, sedation allows the clinician to sustain the focus on caring and to hold to the ethical principle of "alleviating suffering." Whether this is a rationalization or not depends on the individual clinician and her intent. It certainly is more accepted within medical practice at the present time than assisted dying in either of its forms. Moreover, unlike assisted dying, this action has no potential legal repercussions and can therefore be discussed openly. Similarly, partners and family members can maintain the notion that the person died in peace, pain-free, and from "natural" causes. The abruptness of assisted suicide or euthanasia can be avoided, and family members can take their time to adapt to the approach of death.

I have to admit that on first hearing about this practice several years ago, I was angry at what I saw as its inherent dishonesty and at the self-righteous manner in which its supporters defined it as the "answer" to assisted dying. I see very little difference and still feel this anger at times. But I also see sedation as a solution in certain cases where a patient—surrounded by family opposition to assisted death—is suffering intolerably and wants to die. For such a person, this may be the only positive way out of his ordeal, since it allows for the preservation of family unity. I have witnessed these benefits firsthand and, on a few occasions, have even suggested to patients with whom I have worked that they talk with their clinicians about this option.

Nevertheless, part of the problem with terminal sedation is that it is not practiced uniformly in all places. Moreover, there are many clinicians, even within hospice, who refuse to engage in this practice and see no difference between sedation to coma and euthanasia.

A larger problem is that this approach presently lacks guidelines and stringent controls. As one palliative care physician told me, "Legally, I can use this for anyone—a person doesn't have to be dying, or in pain, or even ill." Because the results of terminal sedation are the same as those of assisted dying, I feel that the decision process leading to it should also be controlled. If you are considering sedation in lieu of assisted suicide, I would strongly encourage you to follow the decision process I have outlined here and in Chapter Six.

Specifically, if the patient is not suffering from severe, unrelenting pain, his motives need to be assessed, along with any psychosocial issues, including the possible presence of depression. To bypass this assessment is to ignore the fact that sedation to coma, like assisted suicide, is a deliberate action that has but one direct result—the patient's death.

Questions to Ask Yourself

By now, you have done all that you can, medically speaking, for your patient. You have addressed his physiological concerns to the best of your ability and have made specific referrals as indicated. If your patient is terminal and experiencing intolerable pain or suffering, you have referred him to hospice. Otherwise, you have required that he see a palliative care specialist. You have assessed him for evidence of depression or mental illness, and you may have recommended counseling or treatment. You have also looked at the patient's home situation and are now aware of any pressures being brought to bear on him by his significant others, as well as those individuals' positions on the issue of assisted suicide. Finally, you have discussed with him his full range of options and are absolutely certain of his consistent and unwavering desire for this course of action.

These are the most important patient-related actions you need to take prior to making your final decision. But before proceeding, you would do well to ask yourself:

- Have I done my best to ensure that any problems in communication between my patient and me have been resolved? Am I absolutely certain we fully understand one another?

- Have I provided my patient with every reasonable opportunity to discuss his concerns about his illness and treatment, his fears about death and dying, and his thoughts about assisted dying?

- If am morally opposed to assisted suicide, have I explained the nature of my opposition to my patient? Have I nevertheless convinced him that I will continue to work with him and aggressively respond to his needs?

- Has my opposition to assisted suicide prevented me from working more closely with my patient and fully assessing his motives? Has his desire to die affected the level and type of care I am willing to provide? If so, how can I better assess and attend to his needs?

- Have I clearly communicated to him my uncertainty about assisted suicide, or have I made false assurances that I would likely assist in the future?

- Does my patient fully understand his medical condition and prognosis and the likely outcome of his treatment? Has he exhausted all practical treatment options? Am I certain that further treatment might not improve his quality of life? Does he understand the consequences of refusing additional treatment?

- Am I certain he is not seeking aid in dying as a result of receiving less than adequate care in the past?

- Have I fully and clearly discussed every other option, including those that could hasten his death?

- Have I met my patient's concerns about intractable pain or intolerable suffering with immediate aggressive treatment and referrals? If not, what have been my reasons or motives?

- Have I looked closely at my own skills, beliefs, and fears in the area of aggressive pain control?

- Have I referred my patient to hospice or made hospice a condition for my possible help in the future, if his condition is terminal? If not, have I addressed my own beliefs or prejudices concerning hospice?

- Have I fully addressed all psychosocial issues that might be influencing his decision? If not, what have been my reasons or motives?

- Am I certain he is not being influenced in his decision by family demands, subtle coercion, or economic pressures? Have I really assessed, in depth, the strength of support for his decision from others?

- Have I openly offered to meet with my patient and his significant others to talk about all aspects of his condition and possible treatment options?

- Have I referred him for a psychological or psychiatric assessment or for possible treatment or counseling? If not, what have been my reasons or motives?

- Have I taken any shortcuts in this assessment because of constraints on my time, because of a gut feeling that this is the correct action, or because of an underlying belief that this decision is my patient's alone?

***

Underlying this process of review is the inescapable fact that your patient has asked for your help in dying and may continue to ask. Your response, whether it takes the form of focused dialogue, intensified pain and symptom management, or referrals to hospice or other medical and mental health professionals, may not be enough to satisfy him. His desire to die may continue unabated, and nothing short of sedation and death itself will eliminate his suffering.

If you remain morally opposed to assisted suicide or cannot in good conscience continue to explore the possibility of helping, you need to advise your patient of this, out of compassion and respect for his need to know. He will then be free to make alternative plans, which may mean ending his life in some other way. At this point, your decision-making work will normally be complete. From now on, your focus will be to continue providing compassionate quality care and attending to your patient's physical, emotional, and spiritual needs.

However, if you are still uncertain, or if you are leaning toward providing help, you have a very different task. It is now time to turn inward and assess your motives for continuing along this path. It is also time to look much more closely at the act of assisted suicide, the potential for your further involvement, and the possible effects of helping. These are the topics we will turn to next.

6

The Final Decision

Unless you are opposed to assisted suicide under all circumstances, your work is not yet complete. You may have thoroughly considered your own ethical beliefs about assisted dying, assessed your patient's motives, made all necessary referrals, and done everything you can to ensure the care and comfort of your patient. But before you make any final decision about helping your patient die, it is critical that you now look closely at your own motives for considering this form of help, at the act of assisted suicide itself, and at its possible effects. Only by doing so can you understand why you are considering this decision, what your potential involvement might be, how you might fulfill the task, and what personal and professional risks might still remain.

UNDERSTANDING YOUR OWN MOTIVES

Obviously, there are numerous reasons why clinicians decide to help in their patients' deaths. As is the case when doctors are asked to terminate life support or place a patient in terminal sedation without nutrition, some reluctantly do so in deference to the patient's right or desire to end her suffering. Others, in the words of Dworkin, Nagel, and colleagues, "believe that their most fundamental professional duty is to act in the patient's interests and that, in certain circumstances, it is in their patient's best interests to die."

Physicians with whom I have discussed this have given me a similar range of responses. One clinician, expressing the most common rationale, told me, "On rare occasions it may be the only recourse, when nothing else can be done." A second said, "I believe at some times it really is the practitioner's responsibility, when all quality is gone." Another stated, "It's true that most physical suffering can be controlled, but at what price?" He went on, "There are other kinds of suffering, and sometimes, simply out of mercy, this just makes sense." Talking about hospice patients, one physician explained:

> There are a small number whose pain is both physical and emotional, where one can't be controlled without affecting the other. They're not depressed when they start out, but the restrictions and suffering become too much, and after a while everything is gone, especially their spirit and will to continue. You can medicate them, talk with them, but you can't make it any better for them. They're not going to be changed by their suffering. This is what they want, and you do your best but, in some cases, perhaps it's the right decision.

On the surface, then, the reasons for helping range from professional responsibility to compassion, from the demands of logic to those of emotion. Although I am not a physician, I am certain that there are other reasons, ranging from being worn down by a patient's multiple requests to a desire to maintain control to deeper motivations not consciously known even to the clinician.

Physicians and nursing professionals with whom I have talked have defined professional responsibility in a variety of ways. Some have seen it as maintaining fidelity to the curative model of medicine and never giving up. Others have viewed it as refusing to cross an ethical boundary. Still others have defined it as supporting the patient's autonomy and, above all else, stressing the alleviation of suffering. One physician told me, "If you can no longer help them live, and they're suffering, then it's not out of line to help them die peacefully." Another said, "My task is to care and ease suffering, but needless suffering makes little sense, especially when this [relief] is what they want."

Defining Compassion

The concept of compassion, too, is understood in varying ways, both within our language and in the minds of clinicians. It is characteristically defined as either "suffering together with another" or "being moved by a person's suffering to the point of action aimed at its release."

In the former view, compassion is solely a matter of feeling with the other, establishing a relationship based on emotional sharing. In this sense, it means allowing oneself to identify with the experience of another so that one comes to understand, accept, and respect her. There is a meeting on common ground. I believe this is the meaning that many hospice supporters and opponents of assisted dying have in mind when they describe the compassion involved in much of the psychospiritual work of hospice.

Others are more attuned to the second meaning, "being moved to action by the suffering of another." To them, compassion requires action aimed at mercy or release. It is therefore at the root of both palliative care and many decisions by clinicians to help their patients die. The particular action, however, is controlled by a clinician's ethical sense of appropriate professional behavior.

Only you know how you define your professional duty to your patient and the concept of compassion. And if you are seriously considering assisting in your patient's death, only you know your own primary motives. Are you acting on the basis of professional responsibility as you understand it? Out of compassion or empathy? From a belief in patient autonomy? Or is your decision based on something else entirely? I would recommend that you spend some time looking beneath the surface of your motives, as a variety of thoughts and feelings may be playing a role in your decision.

In contemplating the act of assisting in your patient's death, you may firmly believe that you are motivated by mercy or compassion. If so, you need to ensure that you have an enduring commitment to your decision, that the feeling of compassion is not transient, and that its source is the suffering of your patient and not your own suffering or a past professional or personal experience.

One of the problems with any emotional state, be it love, sorrow, numbness, or empathy, is that it comes in waves. What affects us one moment may not the next, and this depends on a number of factors. Whether you admit it or not, it may not always be easy to leave your personal life at home or to insulate your patient from the effects of your other professional responsibilities. Among the factors that may affect your feelings toward a patient at any particular moment are changes in your personal relationships, sleep patterns, or mood; earlier events of the day; your workload and your level of energy or exhaustion; past or current experiences with comparable patients; and the opportunity simply to talk with this person at length.

If your compassion seems to cool, ask yourself, "What else is going on in my life?" and "Why is my attitude to the patient changing?" Your beliefs and feelings about hastening this person's death need to be consistent and unwavering.

The Dangers of Compassion

A related concern is summed up in the question, "For whom do I really feel compassion?" As M. Scott Peck says of empathy, "With the rarest of exceptions it is only a gift of personal experience." He calls it a "learned phenomenon, forged out of the crucible of one's own real, real pain." If Peck is correct, it is questionable whether anyone who has not encountered physical or emotional suffering similar to that of a patient can comprehend the depth of this person's experience. To see pain in others requires pain in our own history. This truth may raise some self-doubt in younger clinicians, whose experience of suffering is likely to be minimal. This supports the need for a team approach to assisted suicide, the use of professionals, and absolute certainty in the decision to assist.

However, the compassion that arises from our personal acquaintance with pain may reflect either light or shadow. The former is present when we are aware of our own historical encounters with suffering, when we can consciously reflect on them and use them in understanding the suffering of another. The latter, the dark side of compassion, makes itself felt when the root of the emotion is deep in our own unexplored or unconscious suffering or when we project ourselves into the other's experience. Psychologists term this "countertransference." One clinician explained that, for at least a year, he was unaware that he saw his brother's extended and unsuccessful struggle with cancer in any number of his patients.

When I realized this, I didn't view it as wrong, because I thought it helped me become a better doctor. Or so I thought for a time. It was only later, after exhausting myself, [that I saw] that I was trying to save my brother in these other patients. I wasn't responding solely to them and their needs, but to him.

A similar process may be at work when a clinician agrees to help a patient die. One physician told me he knew he was motivated to assist in one case because an earlier patient he had refused to help "went on to die a particularly difficult death" from AIDS. He said, "This death affected me, because he truly was suffering, and I'd refused to help, and nothing short of sedation could've been done." Toward the end, the patient had gone into dementia, and "it was too late to really do anything." He went on to say:

In looking back, I'm certain his death played a role when this other patient, who was very much like him, developed the same conditions and asked for my help. I don't remember seeing the connection at the time, but I do now.

I do not mean to imply that the past always impinges uncon-
sciously on the present, or that any decision you make to help your
patient is somehow less than voluntary on your part. Rather, I am
arguing that you need to take your time and be certain that there
are no ghosts in the room with you and your patient.

A related issue is the type of emotional connection you feel
with your patient and its possible influence on your decision. Compassion and empathy are not boundless or distributed evenly among
vast numbers of potential recipients. They tend to be channeled toward those with whom you feel a particular affinity, though the
issue goes well beyond identification.

Health professionals seldom discuss the psychological components of relationships with patients. You may have been trained to
take a universalistic approach, treating similar patients in the same
manner, applying technical skills, viewing patients first in physiological terms, using scientifically based procedures and protocols for
appraising and responding to their conditions and needs, and maintaining a comfortable distance so as not to compromise your professional judgment or be swayed by sentiment. However, you are
still human and may well find yourself responding with various
emotions to individual patients. There is little wrong with this, as
long as you avoid establishing dual relationships with patients, and
as long as the decisions you make and the quality of the care you
provide are consistent.

The fact is, some patients are more likable than others, or perhaps evoke more positive reactions because of their appearance,
personality, voice, mannerisms, or other characteristics. One patient may also remind you of another, for good or ill.

In deciding whether to hasten a patient's death, therefore, you
might explore what makes one patient appear to be a more suitable
candidate for this option than another. Consider whether it could
be something more than his physical condition and degree of suffering. Might you be identifying with this person? Or does he remind you of someone else for whom you have had warm feelings?
Might you be attempting to complete the incomplete past, to go

back and ease the pain of another you could not help previously, thereby alleviating your own emotional pain or regret? Or does the patient belong to a category of person that you typically respond to more willingly or try to please? Maybe you feel an emotional connection with your patient's significant relation and are moved by this person's emotional pain and plea for intervention even more than you are by your patient's request for assistance.

You might say to yourself that you are leaning toward assisting a particular patient because of her intolerable agony, the lack of feasible options, the support and love of her family, or even her courage in the face of suffering. But there may be some other factor that is predisposing you to help this person. Your task is to determine what that might be. One doctor told me that he asked himself this question again and again after he agreed to help one man and refused another with a similar condition. He found that these had not been straightforward clinical decisions but had been based on something far deeper.

> All the circumstances were right in both cases, but one
> felt more right. For some reason I liked this person, and felt
> closer to him than the other. . . . I don't know why, but it's
> bothered me.

I am not suggesting that any of these factors are all that common, or that you might have difficulty separating your own sentiments from a particular patient's suffering. I am simply pointing out the need to reflect on such possibilities should you find yourself especially moved to help a patient die.

Defining Quality of Life

Related to the concerns we have just examined is the issue of how you might come to define the quality of life of another. It is vital not to project your own notions of suffering and quality onto your patient. In the face of losses that are probably incomprehensible to you, you are in no position to describe the benefits of continued living or the joy the patient might obtain from her few remaining abilities. Nor should you agree to help this person die simply because you would have no interest in surviving if you were in her condition.

The dilemma, however, is that you *are* assessing quality of life, and you need to do so whenever you consider helping a patient die. This is the rub, for you need to establish your own criteria, just as you would for intolerable suffering, and balance them against your patient's idea of quality.

In all of this, it is not necessary to discard your own ideas, but to understand them in relation to possible prejudices. Although you may have established your professional expertise by working with vast numbers of dying patients, you have no right to judge whose life no longer has quality. On the one hand, it is not always possible to fully understand a patient's experience with illness or the depth of her suffering. On the other hand, even a patient devastated by loss of nearly all abilities and racked with pain may still have a sense of quality in intangible possessions, such as the richness of her personal relationships or her spiritual life. Quality is defined by each person individually and is dependent on a range of factors.

Because of these considerations, it is dangerous to use your own notion of quality as a basis for agreeing to help. Your own choice to die under similar circumstances should have little bearing on your decision. This again affirms the preference for a team approach to health care decision making.

Keep in mind that the patient's conception of her quality of life can vary according to her symptoms, the quality of current efforts at palliative care, and any number of psychosocial factors. Also realize that it can be colored by what she hears from you and others. Even your expressed willingness to help may be taken as confirmation of her own negative assessment of her life and may push her farther along this path. To minimize that risk, you must take time in responding to her request and must satisfy yourself that the justification for assisted suicide in this case is objective, enduring, and fully aligned with the patient's deepest values and best interests.

But Who Should Qualify?

So far, I have skirted the issue of who should qualify for a hastened death. I have discussed such issues as intractable pain and intolerable suffering and have alluded to the emotional suffering that may underlie a patient's experience with illness. I have also used terms such as *terminal* and *life-altering* conditions, the latter referring to chronic and incurable illnesses. But nowhere have I clearly stated who should or should not qualify as a subject of assisted suicide. This is because I have seen my task as helping you think clearly about the decision-making process, about the identification of underlying motives, and about responding with care and compassion.

I have my own beliefs about who should qualify, which certainly are implicit throughout this book. To make them only somewhat more explicit, I will say that aid in dying should be reserved for extraordinary cases. At a minimum, I believe that a patient's condition must be incurable and associated with unrelenting and intolerable suffering. I do not see assisted suicide as equivalent to other interventions, particularly when more than one option is available. I believe that the issue needs to be dealt with on a case-by-case basis and answered anew by each clinician, preferably working as part of a health care team or with input from colleagues whenever possible.

Only you can decide if you will draw the line at terminal patients with but weeks or months to live, or if you would also consider patients with chronic and incurable conditions. In reference to this latter group, Peck states:

> I speak of them not because their medical care is necessarily inadequate but to make clear that euthanasia is not solely an issue for hospice-eligible patients. . . . I am not stating the clear belief that the chronically ill should have the right to physician-assisted suicide. . . . I am not saying these people should want euthanasia. What I am saying is that if physician-assisted suicide is to be a right of any rapidly dying patient, the

chronically ill also deserve a hearing when they seek it. Indeed, in order of precedence, I believe they deserve it even before the hospice-eligible terminally ill, who have less time left
to suffer the vicissitudes of their condition.

Similarly, you need to decide whether the suffering that quali-
fies a patient for this option must be exclusively physical or whether
manageable physical suffering combined with extreme emotional
suffering might similarly qualify. But what about existential pain
that might be transitory and, for some, instructional and productive? In the absence of rigid legal distinctions, drawing limits involves a moral decision—one that only you can make.

In the same way, only you can determine the weight you will
give to autonomy in this equation. Although the patient's self-
determination should be a critical consideration, does it override
the issue of your patient's level of suffering? A number of patients
with whom I have discussed this have expressed frustration at their
doctors' hesitation in providing assistance, declaring assisted suicide
to be their ultimate right.

Obviously, some clinicians do agree with this viewpoint. I have
talked with elderly individuals, as well as patients with chronic degenerative conditions, whose clinicians have willingly supplied
them with potentially lethal drugs. One practitioner, who admittedly had not yet faced such a request, shed some light on why a
clinician might respond favorably:

> I can't see any good reason why a strong-willed elderly indi-
> vidual who's lived a fiercely independent life but who's now in
> seriously declining health—with only hospitalization, conva-
> lescent care, a revolving door to the ER, and death to look
> forward to—should not be able to make this decision and be
> helped along in the process.

In the United States, autonomy is certainly the guiding principle of medical care and decision making, but it obviously has its

limits, and the concept can cut two ways. Although you are charged with the ultimate care of your patient, never forget that hastening this person's death against your best judgment jeopardizes your own professional autonomy as a clinician. In reluctantly agreeing to help this individual, you are giving away your own power. You are saying that your needs are less worthy than his. This is something you need to avoid at all costs, not because you must always maintain paternalistic control, but because yielding in this way violates your own personal boundaries and professional principles.

These are all issues you need to consider. In making your decision, I would urge you to look seriously at your own motives and think deeply about your role as a health professional. There is any number of ways to show compassion and caring. Assisted dying may well be one, but there are others that should precede it.

Questions to Ask Yourself

Before proceeding to a final decision, you would do well to ask yourself:

- Have I clearly assessed my own motives? What are my motives? Are they good enough?

- Do I really want to assist my patient in this manner? If not, why am I considering helping? Am I making an objective choice?

- Am I considering assisting because I have been worn down by repeated requests for help, because of my own emotional exhaustion, because I feel pressured, or because I believe my patient's needs are more important than my own?

- Would I help another patient under similar circumstances? If not, what makes this person's request for help different?

- Do I believe I have a duty to provide this option in terminal care? Do I approach such an action willingly, with hesitation, or with reservations?

- Do I experience my patient's request as an emotional imposition? If so, why am I considering assisting?
- What physical conditions should a patient have to receive aid in dying? Have I established my own guidelines? Does this patient qualify?

***

If you have no intention of helping your patient die, you must tell her so and share your reasons openly. She might well benefit from hearing the exact nature of your opposition or concerns, even perhaps gaining personal insight from the dialogue. For example, if your opposition is deeply spiritual, your refusal may prompt her to think about and discuss such matters. Indeed, it may help her become conscious of the existential and spiritual forces that lie at the root of her request.

If you are still deliberating, or are leaning toward aiding your patient, you need to begin thinking in far more detail about the act itself and what it would entail. This will involve sharing your thoughts with other professionals, eliciting information, assessing what you hear, and considering your innermost thoughts, feelings, and needs. I would advise you to make no final decision to help until you have

- Established the enduring, unwavering nature of the patient's desire to die
- Discovered all that this patient expects of you
- Determined the absolute limit of involvement with which you are comfortable and the degree to which you are emotionally and practically prepared
- Obtained a full understanding of the patient's plan for his death so that you can assess the probability of success and the potential for psychic harm to others who may be involved, including yourself

- Assessed the potential professional risks that might accompany such an action
- Considered the emotional effects of such an action on yourself

THOUGHTS ABOUT THE PROCESS OF ASSISTING

Discussion of assisted suicide at professional gatherings, training sessions, and meetings of bioethics committees presents little problem to most clinicians. I have attended countless such conclaves and seen physicians, nurses, social workers, psychologists, and clergy relish the theoretical and ethical dilemmas that are raised. The exchange of ideas, safely removed from real patients, ranges freely over a broad theoretical and practical front. However, attention is usually confined to ethics and broad options. Even when majority opinion is supportive of a medically hastened death, participants, almost to a person, actively avoid the question "How is this done?" Perhaps some already know. But it is clear that others do not want to know or do not want to make the discussion too real. There may also be a fear that either the question or the answer will confer a measure of "guilt" in the eyes of colleagues—one must be thinking about helping a patient die or must already have done so.

Meanwhile, the clinicians who do help often make mistakes, either with drugs and dosages or in the final process of decision making. They may fail, for example, to forge a complete understanding with the patient about the manner of death, or they may ignore key factors and possible effects. Mistakes may occur because the clinician is unaware of all the complexities of the process, beginning with the decision itself and ending with the patient's death. Such lack of knowledge exists because of the secrecy that surrounds the practice. Under these circumstances, each assisted death is a new venture. To help reduce the likelihood of uninformed decisions and the mistakes they produce, I will now outline the basic features of the process.

The Persistence of the Request

The decision and caring process described in the previous chapter is predicated on your receiving a firm request from your patient for aid in dying. You may have had a few conversations with him about his desires, the issues that are affecting his decision, the course of his treatment, and other options. And during this time he may have made additional requests. In most cases, as you respond directly to the patient's concerns and fears, his certainty about assisted death will gradually dissolve. In the few cases where this does not occur, you may feel pressured to state when your final decision will be made. For example, the patient may say, "Since nothing's really working, and I'm still suffering, how long before you know whether you'll help?"

Because we are talking about an act that stands outside of the law and standards of clinical practice, you may not know the answer to this question. Nevertheless, compassion and respect demand that your patient receive a response. Although it would seem best that your decision come slowly and thoughtfully, when a patient is near death or his suffering is obviously unmanageable, that response should not be too long delayed. If you have completed the preceding process and exhausted or ruled out other options, if you are supportive of the idea, and if the patient meets your criteria, the time would seem right to talk in detail about his expectations and to begin the process that I outline in the remainder of this chapter.

It might be useful here to consider some of the guidelines for assisted suicide that have been published in various medical and law journals over the past several years. Without exception, all have argued that the request for assisted dying needs to be enduring, consistent, and without any sign of serious hesitation.

A few guidelines also specify a minimum waiting period during which the request must be repeated. This serves as a safeguard against impulsivity and the possibility that a patient will change his mind. Waiting periods of varying lengths have been suggested in legislative initiatives on behalf of assisted suicide. Oregon's Death with Dignity Act, for example, which was approved by voters in 1994 but repealed by the state legislature and placed on the November 1997 ballot, specifies a fifteen-day period between oral requests. The second request is to be followed by a witnessed written directive and a further forty-eight-hour wait before a physician can provide a prescription. The Model State Act drafted by Baron and others requires a fourteen-day interval between requests.

By contrast, a proposal by the (San Francisco) Bay Area Network of Ethics Committees suggests three requests, the first two separated by at least forty-eight hours and the third taking place at the time the prescription is issued. The authors have structured the proposal for clinicians, not voters, and have designed it especially to meet the needs of a more restricted group of patients, those who are suffering intolerably and close to death.

The demand for consistent multiple requests over a reasonable period of time is prudent, as impulsivity is a serious risk. The patient's continuing appeal for a hastened death should be a critical component in your final decision. As you address his concerns, you should be alert to any signs of wavering.

If you have followed the procedure outlined in this book, the idea of a waiting period should not be objectionable to you. Except in very rare cases, I would suggest that the minimum be the time it takes you to complete the tasks I have outlined. This could be several days or weeks, more time being needed if you make a referral to hospice, other types of palliative care, mental health assessment, counseling, or psychiatric treatment.

Obviously, if the patient is near death, or suffering intolerably despite palliative care, your decision period should be shorter. By contrast, if a person's request is based on a number of factors—including, for example, fear of future conditions—it would seem best to continue working with him for some time, using a variety of approaches.

In using terms such as *enduring* and *consistent*, I do not mean to imply that a patient must never, even for a moment, show the slightest signs of reconsidering his decision after he has made his initial request. Nor am I suggesting that he must be so convinced of his choice that he would end his life immediately on receiving a prescription. An enduring request is one that points to a continuity of belief and increasing certainty over time. No doubt there will be some wavering, but it should be minimal and should progressively diminish. Though there is likely to be hesitation over the final timing of death, the desire to have the choice remains firm.

What I have learned from numerous patients is that the possession of lethal medications often represents the assurance of a way out. Such patients may not avail themselves of this opportunity for a very long time, if at all, even though they may be suffering severely. They wait until every other condition in their life seems right. This occurred in the case of Diane, reported by Timothy Quill in the *New England Journal of Medicine*, where months passed between his writing of a lethal prescription and her death. Similarly, in a 1992 article, Howard Brody wrote:

> The normal human response to facing the final moment before death, when one has control over the choice, ought to be ambivalence. The bottle of pills allows full recognition of that ambivalence: I, the patient, can sleep on it, and the pills will still be there in the morning; I do not lose my means of escape through the delay.

The possibility that the day may never come when the patient takes the medication should not make you any less committed to helping him die. Nor should it make you cavalier about providing this option. You would do well to treat such a decision in the same manner as you would the act of euthanasia, as it carries the overwhelming potential to indeed be final.

The Problems with Waiting

If you delay too long before denying a patient's request, or if you fail to specify your concerns and your limits, you may lead a patient to assume too much. This can have serious consequences should the patient be left with insufficient time to seek aid from another clinician. In such a case, the patient may threaten to use more violent means to achieve her death, saying, "I'd really like a prescription, but if I can't get it, I'll just have to take matters into my own hands. I don't like violence, but I've got to do something."

The risk you run in delaying too long does not lie only in the possibility of a violent act. Your patient and her significant others may instead choose to "quietly" take matters into their own hands. Such patients may make use of whatever means are available, thereby increasing the potential for failure. As I documented in *Final Acts of Love*, the true causes and circumstances of many of these assisted suicides are successfully hidden by family members and other participants. Official records typically list them as natural deaths.

Significant others, acting out of a sense of obligation, may thus become far more involved than they had ever planned or desired. Using prescriptions they happen to have in their possession, or even street drugs, at doses of unknown lethality, they may watch their loved ones die slowly if they die at all. At the expected time of death, they are often left terrified and confused about what to do next. Several partners and family members I interviewed told of being alone with an unconscious person in the middle of the night, hours after the person had ingested a supposed lethal dose. They frequently spoke of turning desperately to other drugs, "lethal" injections, or plastic bags that would asphyxiate the person. Some even risked all and called 911, contrary to the explicit instructions of the patient, who may have told them when the act was being planned, "Don't let me wake up."

Knowing that this threat exists, however, should never force you to agree to help a patient die. Instead, it should convince you of the need to provide her with your full emotional support and the very best care possible and to convey your decision to her as soon as you are certain. Obviously, compassion enters the equation, but you need to follow your own heart, even given the threat of violent suicide or of a potentially disastrous "homemade" assisted death.

The Patient's Expectations

As I pointed out in Chapter Three, before you agree to help your patient die, it is critical to understand exactly what she is asking of you. By now, you know the difference between the statements "I'd like a prescription to end my life" and "I'd like you to give me something when it gets bad." At first, you may have had no way of knowing whether she was asking for a promise to be kept out of pain or an assurance of your help in dying. But as a result of working with her, you should be certain of what she desires.

Nevertheless, even after you have discussed your patient's request, her motives, and your willingness to consider assisting in her death, you may still be unclear whether she is asking for a lethal prescription or for your more direct involvement should she be unable to end her own life. Even a simple statement such as "I'd like you to give me something . . ." is ambiguous. You must immediately respond, "What exactly are you asking me to do?"

Similarly, you need to consider whether you have been absolutely clear in all of your communications with your patient. Did you tell her: "We need to talk about this in detail. I need to work with you to address your immediate concerns, and I need to think about this before I make any final decision"? Or did you say: "Don't worry, I'll do everything necessary so you won't suffer"? Although the latter is hardly a promise of assisted suicide, I have talked with more than a few patients over the years who, hearing these words, thought their clinicians had given them just that assurance. Most found out too late that they were wrong.

However you respond, you would be wise to ask your patient if she fully understands your meaning. You might say, "I really want to avoid any chance of being misinterpreted. Can you tell me what you think I said?"

Conversely, if you do not discuss with her all aspects of her request, you may well misunderstand her words and fail to grasp her underlying expectations. Before you agree to assist a patient in her death, it is essential that you understand how extensive your role might be. For example, you need to know whether she expects you

- To provide a prescription for a potentially lethal drug
- To be on call as well for consultation by phone in the event of an emergency
- To administer other medications if she is unable to do so on her own or if the oral medications fail to cause death in a reasonable period of time
- To sign the death certificate specifying that she died as a result of natural causes, regardless of your involvement in her death

Each of these possibilities has its own ethical ramifications and carries its own risks.

Providing the Means to Die

Before you agree to provide your patient with a prescription for a potentially lethal drug, you must look into the possible complications that might ensue for your patient, as well as into the precise effects of different medications and dosages. The type of medication you will be considering is likely to be stringently controlled, and you need to feel completely confident not only about its suitability to the task but also about its subsequent defensibility in the event of an investigation.

When the demise of the patient is the goal, a conservative approach to prescription—that is, the choice of a less strictly controlled substance—is likely to be counterproductive. A medication of uncertain lethality poses the risk of leaving the patient alive and in a significantly worse state. A further important consideration in selecting a drug is its probable side effects given the patient's specific condition. Control for nausea and vomiting is vital.

In my interviews with significant others who had participated in assisted deaths, I was told of several cases where doctors prescribed drugs such as Percocet because they were fearful of using almost certainly lethal barbiturates such as Seconal or Nembutal. Their patients survived. In a few instances, even intermediate opioids were ineffective, and patients suffered severe effects from the acetaminophen or aspirin contained in them. Interviewees described cases where patients survived massive doses of Valium, Vicodin, and even strong opioids like Roxanol and MS Contin. (This last drug may have failed in some instances because of morphine tolerance.)

Clinicians cannot be blamed for such results when the information they need to manage assisted suicide is ignored in medical schools and professional journals because of the illegality of assisted suicide. They are to blame, however, when their prescribing of inappropriate medications or dosages is due to personal fear of investigation or lack of effort to research the most effective medications for this purpose.

If you do not have the necessary information, where would you go to find it? Outside of a few stories of assisted deaths in the Netherlands or documented by a small group of suicidologists and right-to-die activists, few have collected concise data on fatal dosages. And the information that has been gathered is questionable, in that it is typically based on anecdotal evidence that is not always trustworthy. You might be inclined to consult the *Physicians' Desk Reference*. However, although lethal dosages for a broad range of medications are listed there, you first need to know where to look. Also, the figures tend to be conservative, to prevent any risk of overdose. In some cases, even when clinicians have doubled the stated minimum lethal dose, death has not resulted.

Patients are not to blame for failures. After all, they are not medical professionals or chemists. What some can be faulted for, however, is treating their clinicians merely as drug suppliers, demanding the wrong medications by name or expecting their physicians to know what substance to use. More than a few patients have told me they knew that a lethal pill existed because they had seen it in the news or a film or read about it in a spy novel.

Then there are the patients who pride themselves on having bought Derek Humphry's best-selling "suicide manual," *Final Exit*, but have little knowledge even of what they have read. This widely available book has lifted the overall level of public knowledge on the subject and has been responsible for several highly publicized suicides and assisted deaths, a few of them infamous. Nevertheless, the author's inclusion of a number of less lethal drugs seems questionable, even though readers are advised to use them only in conjunction with a plastic bag for purposes of asphyxiation. As I have described in *Final Acts of Love*, however, such a death is undignified, and it places an unnecessary emotional and legal burden on significant others who witness or participate in it.

I can only advise you never to trust a patient's interpretation of such material. If he asks you for a specific drug and dosage, I would encourage you to ask where he got this information and then conduct your own investigation. To do anything less is a prescription for failure and grief.

Remember that half-measures do no good. Your goal, in most instances, is to enable the patient to have a peaceful and dignified death. There can be no peace in failure or loss of organ function. If you are going to help, do so in a way that minimizes the risk of mistakes.

The Potential for Further Involvement

If a prescription fails, you may be asked to help more directly in bringing about the patient's death. It is important that you consider this possibility prior to making your final decision.

Any potential conflict between your own needs and the demands of your patient should be identified in advance. If you agree to help, you must make clear to your patient what you will and will not do, emphasizing that these limits will apply whatever may transpire during his attempt to end his life.

Many of the people I interviewed who had participated in the assisted deaths of partners or family members told me they had become more deeply involved than they had planned. They expressed their regret that they had given no thought to a "backup plan." Confident that the drugs prescribed or collected for this purpose would work, they were unprepared for failure.

In many cases where a clinician provided a prescription, significant others told me they would have wished for a doctor or nurse to be available to receive an emergency call in the event something went wrong. Their need would have been, first, for information, assurance, emotional support, or advice, and then for either additional medication that could be injected or direct intervention by the clinician.

Such actions entail vexing personal and ethical dilemmas. The few clinicians I have talked to about the issue of extended involvement have not been in consensus. Even those who confessed to prescribing medications and to having been on call at least once for such an event had varying opinions. One who told me that he had helped more than twenty patients die said he had "no qualms" about further involvement when this was necessary. As he put it, "I knew this was part of the bargain when I agreed to help." However, another said giving advice "to a stranger over the phone" made him "feel like a murderer." A third told me that he had agreed to go to the home if there were an emergency, but "didn't want to, and didn't ever believe it would be necessary." Unfortunately, sometimes it is.

Being on call also means that you are aware of the timing of the patient's attempt at suicide. Some clinicians would prefer not to have this knowledge. Without it, they can still feel, in one physician's words, on "the edge of innocence." Further, if you agree with your patient on a particular time when you would be available, he may feel less freedom to postpone the final act. The obvious solution would be to provide him with your schedule, along with phone and pager numbers, so as to leave open several windows of opportunity.

The Question of Euthanasia

The potential for further involvement brings up the issue of euthanasia. As opinion polls of health care professionals attest, many clinicians feel far less comfortable with this subject than with that of assisted suicide.

Right-to-die supporters often argue that the potential for failure in assisted suicide is what makes euthanasia a more attractive option—at least for them. They also maintain that it may be the only option left for patients with incurable illnesses who have waited too long for oral medications and who have lost their ability to act alone or to swallow. They further point out that patients suffering from severe nausea and vomiting, symptoms that are common in late-stage cancer, cannot avail themselves of assisted suicide.

In assessing the acceptability of euthanasia, it is helpful to compare the practice with the double effect of high-dose morphine. The latter is widely supported because the claimed intent is to alleviate pain, not to cause death. A somewhat similar distinction is drawn between euthanasia and assisted suicide: though both actions may result in death, one is more certain and final than the other.

Euthanasia leaves no ambiguity about your involvement. The patient's death is your primary intent, it is undeniably caused by your actions—albeit at the request of the patient—and it occurs immediately. Further, the dominance of your role is mirrored by the passivity of the patient. Some of the greatest risks of this practice arise from the fact that the patient is deprived of total control of her dying.

By contrast, when a doctor provides a patient a potentially lethal prescription, the possibility remains that it will serve only as "insurance" and will never be used. It is this uncertainty that provides clinicians with the semblance of innocence. If the prescription is used days, weeks, or even months later, the clinician is removed from the act—in terms of time, place, and causation.

This choice between assisted suicide and euthanasia is a morally difficult one, as there are positive and negative aspects of each practice. Assisted suicide can help you maintain distance from the event itself, and it places more control in the hands of the patient. The distance helps sustain the pretense that your work with your patient is only of a curative or palliative nature.

Commenting on the preference for assisted suicide over euthanasia in a 1992 article, Howard Brody says:

> It is not preferable because the physician is less directly involved as a causal agent; letting the patient do the dirty work

can be an abrogation of responsibility rather than an exercise in professional integrity. Instead, the preference lies in the potentially therapeutic effect of both having the means to end one's life and having personal control over the time and setting of their use.

I would add that the lack of direct involvement, however, may prevent you from fully realizing the impact of the action, for good or ill. Perhaps only by directly apprehending it can you realize its awesome nature and appreciate the true significance of your decision. Whether or not you look at this way, you are helping a patient to suicide.

The Power of Your Presence

If you are considering assisting your patient's death, you must be prepared for all eventualities and must feel absolutely comfortable with the idea that you might be present in the room when it occurs. If your patient's suicide attempt is likely to take place at home, you should learn as much as you can about his plans, about who might be in attendance, and whether they all fully support his decision to die. (If you have worked with your patient for some time on this decision and have discussed such support with the patient's significant others, as I suggested in Chapter Four, then this will be unnecessary.)

There are patients who orchestrate their deaths so as to be surrounded by friends and family members. This is especially the case among AIDS patients, where an individual may be supported at the end by both a family of choice and his family of origin. Given the current illegal status of assisted death in the United States and in most other areas of the world, be aware that agreeing to be either on call or present may place you at some personal risk.

Providing help from a distance is far less of a risk. A person ingesting dual-purpose drugs that you have prescribed weeks earlier is very different from one who dies in your presence under the scrutiny of others you have never met and have no reason to trust. The presence of a single recalcitrant family member who has been opposed to this decision multiplies the risk that you will later be held responsible for the patient's death.

Not only do you need to feel entirely comfortable with the setting and with those in attendance, you should also make certain that anyone who may be present is both informed and emotionally prepared for what may occur. You should not agree to help before you are satisfied on this point. You would also do well to warn your patient against any casual discussion of his plans for an assisted suicide or of your possible involvement. You should emphasize the very private nature of such an act and his need to protect you and others who might be in attendance.

Another risk to be concerned about is that if you undertake to be present at the time of the suicide, the patient may look on any visit by you—particularly if such visits are rare—as an opportunity to end his life. And if you have come specifically for this purpose, he may feel constrained to follow through, despite last-minute misgivings, out of gratitude and respect for your "valuable time." As Howard Brody stated in his 1992 article:

> If I am terminally ill of cancer in the Netherlands and summon my family physician to my house to administer the fatal dose, I am powerfully motivated to deny any ambivalence I may feel. Wavering at this last minute may forever label me as inconsistent and hence no longer available for euthanasia under the official guidelines. Also, I have called my doctor away from his or her family to come to my bedside; I would feel both foolish and impolite were I to change my mind now that he or she has arrived.

If you make the decision to assist in your patient's death or to provide emotional or therapeutic support, you need to be fully cognizant of the power that your presence conveys. The patient is very much like a hesitant bridegroom at the church door, whose serious second thoughts may be pushed aside as he looks at the assemblage of invited guests. Whether you are a physician, nursing professional, social worker, or therapist, your presence in itself may provide the momentum for this act to proceed, as your patient may be loath to "disappoint" you.

To avoid this dynamic, you need to establish an honest and caring relationship with your patient—one without professional distance or an obvious power differential. An emphasis on shared decision making throughout the treatment process can do much to instill a sense of power in the patient. When you go to his home at the time appointed for the act of suicide, it is important to make clear that you are willing to come back again if he has any uncertainty about proceeding. This declaration will carry more weight if you have already made more than one home visit, so I strongly recommend that you do so as a matter of routine practice.

Needless to say, your presence before or during an assisted suicide does not always have to carry a negative potential. If you have a close, supportive, caring relationship with your patient, his seeing you may afford him the comfort of your professionalism and the sense that nothing will go wrong. In fact, with this in mind, some have argued that it is ethically imperative for a clinician to attend a patient's assisted suicide. And in its 1994 policy statement "Client Self-Determination in End-of-Life Decisions," the National Association of Social Workers said, "If legally permissible, it is not inappropriate for a social worker to be present during an assisted suicide if the client requests the social worker's presence."

Your Role in Declaring Cause of Death

A final consideration is whether you will agree to sign the death certificate and state that the patient died as a result of the underlying illness. This will allow the patient's family to call the mortuary and arrange to have her body removed without the involvement of authorities. There are many clinicians who refuse to provide a patient with a potentially lethal prescription but do agree to sign a death certificate to help the patient's family avoid an official coroner's investigation, autopsy, ruling of suicide, or even criminal indictment of those who have assisted in the death.

Regardless of their knowledge or suspicions about the actual cause of death, there are many physicians who see a refusal to sign as placing an unnecessary burden on others, given that the patient acted solely in response to a terminal illness and intolerable suffering. As one doctor told me:

> It really is no one's business whether this is a suicide or a death from cancer or AIDS. Yes, I've signed off on a few of these cases, to protect the family and the patient's reputation. It wasn't a matter of wanting to hide the cause from the life insurance company or to defraud them in any way.

A slightly more conservative—though still compassionate—approach was described to me by an internist with a large AIDS caseload. He claimed that he had never assisted one of his patients, had never been asked to knowingly sign such a death certificate, and preferred "being kept in the dark" about how his hospice patients actually died. Nevertheless, he said that he "would probably still agree to sign, just on principle." As he saw it: "A patient may end his life, maybe even with the morphine I gave him for pain, but the disease is the real cause of his death, and would've killed him anyway."

There is an obvious practical motivation in agreeing to sign if you are at least indirectly responsible for the patient's death. Doing so can usually protect you from any further risks related to your role in the patient's death. If you fail to sign, and the death is ruled a possible suicide or assisted suicide, there is a chance, albeit slight, that you will be investigated. This is a particular risk if authorities place pressure on significant others to describe what really happened. To sign in order to avoid such a hazard may seem self-serving, but this rationale is common. Of 140 assisted deaths that I studied, only 15 were officially ruled to be suicides. The rest were either knowingly or unknowingly covered up by physicians.

This is certainly an ethical issue you will have to consider. If you have agreed to help someone die, you need to ponder whether this further action on your part is an extension of that agreement. Like assisted suicide itself, signing a false death certificate is criminal, and your choice will therefore be dictated by your conscience, as well as by the practical considerations I have discussed. From an ethical point of view, such an act is undoubtedly more acceptable if its purpose is to reduce the emotional burden on a patient's survivors.

As far as logistics are concerned, you should be certain that your patient's significant others know when and how they can reach you in the event of death. If they do not, serious problems can arise. In one case I studied, a patient's two clinicians both agreed in advance to sign his death certificate, even though neither consented to help him die. On the night of his death, his partner, who had assisted him in a particularly horrendous suicide, could locate neither doctor. The result, as he described, was needless emotional agony:

> I was finally connected to a second backup who told me he wouldn't sign anything, and that I should call 911. . . . I told them I thought [my partner] was dead, but they arrived in full force only ten minutes later. I hopped in the back [of the ambulance], and they began working on him. One turned to the other and said, "I think I got a pulse." That did it. I began to cry, and I said, "Please, just let him die." They looked at me, and then stopped working on him. . . . Later, after he was declared dead, one of the coroner's people asked me a few simple questions and then said that it looked like [a suicide].

The Need for Follow-Up

An issue that is seldom discussed in the literature on assisted suicide is the emotional care of a patient's survivors. This apparent lack of focus on the well-being of others is to be expected, given the emphasis in medicine on the patient-doctor relationship. But when a patient dies, the family is too often cut off and left alone to pick up the burden. The obvious exception here is the work done by hospice, where the patient is seen as part of a larger unit. Hospice typically provides psychospiritual support and bereavement counseling for those impacted by the patient's death. However, even if your patient is receiving hospice care, this does not necessarily mean that survivors can openly discuss the actual cause of her death.

Outside of hospice, the issue is much more serious. If there is only one survivor, such as a spouse, this person may have no one with whom to talk, to express concerns, second thoughts, or possible regrets about the choice of an assisted death. An assisted suicide can leave such a survivor feeling particularly alone.

This is one of the reasons I strongly recommend not helping a patient die without complete support for the decision from family and other significant relations. They need to have time early on to think deeply about their own concerns, to share them openly with the patient, and to come to a sense of peace with the decision. Family or couple counseling during the decision period can facilitate this process, as well as provide a basis for continuing emotional support after the death of the patient. Such a resource will prove critical in the event that there is difficulty with the patient's death or if the survivor became more involved in it than previously planned. Indeed, the failure of the prescribed medication to cause a patient's death in a reasonable period of time has often resulted in such further involvement. This places an unnecessary emotional and potential legal burden on these significant relations. Because of this potential, their emotional needs should not be ignored.

Why am I mentioning this? If you help the patient die, you will also have helped end this relationship. Although your primary responsibility is to the patient, your participation in her death would seem to imply a responsibility for the emotional and spiritual well-being of those most intimately affected by it. Such endings can be good or bad. Difficult emotional repercussions may be avoided if the patient's assisted death is seen by others as necessary, if everyone has had the opportunity to say goodbye and to share his or her individual struggle with the decision, and if all parties have been able to resolve long-standing interpersonal issues. On the other hand, if the decision-making process has been one-sided, if the patient provided few opportunities for closure, and if conflict is still festering, the bereavement process may be harrowing.

You can help ensure the more favorable of these outcomes by being certain, before you make your final decision, that conflict is at a minimum, that resolution has been attempted, and that your patient and her significant relations are knowledgeable of community resources and bereavement services, including pastoral counseling and other forms of spiritual support. You might cover some of these points in a family meeting during the decision period. The need for support is a strong reason for choosing the hospice option, even if the patient decides on an assisted death.

I suggest also that, whether or not you were present at the death, you make personal contact soon afterward with the patient's family or significant other. A simple follow-up phone call or a home visit, conveying that someone cares, can prevent survivors from feeling abandoned in their greatest time of need.

Making such a connection may also reduce the personal and professional risks you could face should it emerge that a significant relation was less than fully supportive of the patient's assisted death. Studies of cases involving potential medical malpractice have shown that the risk of lawsuits from patients or family members is reduced by the clinician's thoughtful consideration, respect, and communication. I imagine that the same might apply here.

Such pragmatic issues aside, the central question is whether you believe that your duty extends beyond your patient and beyond the act of prescribing a potentially lethal prescription. Wisdom and compassion would seem to imply that it does.

Questions to Ask Yourself

- Am I absolutely certain the patient's request is consistent and enduring? If not, do I understand the source of any hesitation?

- Am I absolutely certain that my expressed potential willingness to help has not been taken as confirmation of my patient's own negative assessment of her quality of life and has not affected her own final decision to end her life?

- Do I understand exactly what my patient expects of me? Am I certain no additional involvement might be required? Am I comfortable with this role?

- Is my patient physically capable of performing this act alone? What if she fails? Would I feel comfortable being available by phone in the event of an emergency, and going to her home if necessary?

- If I have not thought through the ramifications of further involvement, why have I not done so? Do I view such involvement as ethical?

- Have I carefully considered which medications I might prescribe, taking into account the nature of the patient's condition? Am I confident that she can take the prescription, and that it would work?

- Has she described her plans to me and told me who might be with her at her death? If I agree to be present, how can I be certain that others who might be there fully support her decision?

- Would I be willing to sign my patient's death certificate? What might be my motivation for covering up the actual cause of death?

- Have I given thought to how I might help the patient's family or significant others deal with her assisted suicide?

PROFESSIONAL AND PERSONAL RISKS

Because assisted suicide is illegal almost everywhere in the world, it exposes you to both professional and personal risks, as well as a number of ethical dilemmas. You may be prosecuted or sanctioned for participating in such a death, and you may even lose your professional license. This is why those who help patients die do so privately, secretly, underground.

The environment of secrecy, which denies you opportunities to openly discuss these decisions and actions with colleagues, also greatly increases the risk of error, of making the wrong decision. There are no clinical practice guidelines to give you direction, nor are there hospital policies or ethics committees to which you can turn for advice. Assisted suicide, unlike sedation to coma or withdrawal of life-sustaining equipment, is not seen as a "treatment" decision. Its status is that of an outlaw. Until it moves into the realm of legally approved acts, you effectively are on your own.

Before you make any final decision on helping your patient die, it would therefore be wise to look briefly at a few of the professional and personal risks involved, as well as at some related issues.

The Risk of Others Who Know

If you fail to take into account the attitudes of significant others to assisted suicide, you run a risk of reprisal by an emotionally distraught survivor. The person may be morally opposed to the practice in all cases or may simply believe that the final decision was made too soon. The possibility of a punitive reaction is especially marked when a patient and her significant relations had unfinished business between them, unresolved anger or guilt, or strong religious differences. The incensed family member might inform legal authorities of your participation in the suicide or even file a civil lawsuit against you for wrongful death.

Admittedly, there have been no such lawsuits to date, and in North America and Great Britain over the past several years, the number of clinicians indicted on these grounds has been negligible. Even the involvement of Timothy Quill in Diane's death, made public by his own "confession" in print, failed to result in a grand jury indictment. Other clinicians who have told similar stories in numerous newspaper articles over the past few years have been largely ignored by state and medical licensing authorities. The only exception has been the high-profile acts of Kevorkian in Michigan, but despite his participation in more than fifty known deaths, he has yet to be convicted—or sued by family members in civil court.

There seem to be two related reasons for this lack of criminal and civil action. First, most assisted suicides emerge out of the private clinician-patient relationship and are carried out either by the patient alone or in the company of a few supportive family members or friends. Second, most of these deaths result from the prescribing of "dual purpose" medications, which make it quite difficult to prove that the clinician intended to help the patient die.

Moreover, families and significant others tend to stay silent. This is particularly true when they themselves have been involved in some way, but silence is also a means to avoid the stigma of suicide and to protect unknowing family members from the truth. Clearly, significant relations have not been the leading forces in instigating investigations of clinicians who have helped a family member die.

Risks can also arise when a clinician's involvement becomes known to strangers in the patient's circle of friends. In a poignant series on clinicians and assisted suicide that ran several years ago in the *Boston Globe*, journalist Dick Lehr described the story of "Dr. Green," who had "made the pledge" to help ensure the death of his patient, a man in the late stages of AIDS. A week after prescribing a month's supply of barbiturates along with "a pain narcotic," Green received the call. The patient told him the time had arrived, then asked him to come to his home.

> Several of the patient's friends were at his house when Green arrived that evening. "I didn't talk to him about why he did it in this particular way and am kind of curious now and wish I had," says Green about the surreal evening to come. "He said goodbye to everybody, and it wasn't a big deal, again, because he'd done a lot of goodbyes."

The patient summoned Green upstairs with him. "He wanted me to come up with him," says Green. They talked. His patient put on music, a short requiem by the French composer Gabriel Fauré. "There was no struggle or agony to it, just a very comfortable thing." They said goodbye and thanked each other and hugged. Then the man drank all the pills with water, and then he drank the narcotic.

Although such an act potentially placed this clinician in harm's way, Green made no mention of being outraged at finding a house full of strangers. In fact, "Green stayed on for awhile that night to talk with his patient's friends and family." At the memorial service, however, Green began to worry about being found out and arrested. But he made no mention of the risk of "blackmail," in the form of requests for help from any of the several friends present that night who may have been similarly suffering from AIDS. I do know of patients in the San Francisco Bay Area who have changed doctors specifically because of this new-found knowledge. One patient told me about his first meeting with his new physician: "I explained to him that I'd heard good things about him, that he was a good doctor, and compassionate, in that he'd helped a close friend of mine die." Obviously, you would do well to talk with your patient about this potential problem.

The lack of criminal and civil court action buoys my belief that clinicians, for the most part, are cautious in making such decisions, typically providing help only in safe situations, where a patient's suffering is intolerable and family support is firm. (However, whether or not to include significant others in your deliberations solely because of fear of exposure would be wrong. I believe that the needs of extremely close significant relations should never be ignored.)

The relative lack of prosecutions and lawsuits should in no way make you any less vigilant about the overall quality of your decision making. Even with growing public acceptance of the idea of assisted suicide, I would urge you to still treat this action as an extraordinary last resort, particularly given the increasing vociferousness of its opponents. Remember, too, that you may be sued for malpractice. Such suits might allege that your provision of assistance was inappropriate and ill-advised in light of the patient's medical condition, prognosis, and psychological state, or that the request was fulfilled "too early" in the dying process or was motivated by nonmedical factors beyond your area of expertise.

Risk and Confidentiality

A related issue that runs throughout any talk of professional risk is confidentiality. Professional ethics are designed to protect the patient from any unauthorized disclosure by his clinician. Thus, as long as the patient is rational and competent, the clinician is generally prohibited from divulging any information about his case, even to family members.

This is not an absolute rule. If a patient is a potential suicide, the laws in most jurisdictions, and the ethical standards of most professional associations, require that health care staff inform appropriate authorities, thereby triggering an intervention. This typically takes the form of temporary placement in a psychiatric facility, where assessments are made of the risk of suicide and of the patient's mental competence.

Nevertheless, even many within hospice who are opposed to assisted suicide rarely respond in this manner, and certainly not on the patient's initial request for aid in dying. The claims of opponents notwithstanding, there is increasing belief in the rationality of assisted suicide for the terminally ill. Staff in many hospice programs, rather than having to take what they themselves formerly saw as draconian measures to prevent suicide, are typically required to inform other members of the care team while continuing to work closely with the patient in positive ways. This serves to alert team members to the risk, prepares them to mobilize additional resources to meet the patient's needs, and allows them to consider the potential for crisis intervention. Throughout, patient confidentiality is maintained: no one outside of the care team—even a significant other—is told of the patient's desire unless the patient gives permission. To do so would be divisive. Instead, staff strongly urge patients to discuss their concerns with their family members.

Staff use this approach because they fear that a breach of confidence could rupture the trust they have established with the person and bring dialogue to a halt, thereby jeopardizing chances of preventing the suicide. Only if the risk of suicide becomes immediate do staff reconsider this position. But even then, as one hospice social worker told me,

> This doesn't mean we're going to take a patient out of his home and place him in a facility to keep him from ending his life. That would be absolutely ridiculous, especially when the patient's dying anyway. This is the last thing a person needs who's already lost everything and is fighting hard for whatever dignity remains.

Only in rare cases, or as a result of a suicide attempt, may confidentiality be breached and family members informed of the patient's intent. In such an instance, medications in the home are more closely monitored.

It is important to bear in mind that where there is family conflict over a patient's desire to die, confidentiality serves two distinct functions, which give rise to their own particular ethical dilemmas. First, it ensures that the patient can carry out his plans without interference. The dilemma here is whether to protect that freedom or to take into account the needs of significant others.

Second, confidentiality is your personal shield against charges of wrongdoing. You therefore need to question your motives for secrecy, asking yourself, "Who am I protecting, the patient or myself?" The issue will become real when a family member contacts you to express concern about a patient's well-being or the risk of suicide. Do you agree to talk with this person but dismiss her concerns, covering up the plans you have made with your patient? Remember that she may have information you need to properly assess the patient. One possible solution to this dilemma is to talk with this person about her concerns, using this discussion as an opportunity to learn more about your patient.

Another dilemma is that there may be times when a patient, though an unlikely candidate for your help, nevertheless informs you of his intention to end his own life. In such a case, the moment may come when you feel the need to breach confidentiality in order to protect the patient from an ill-advised act. This is a judgment call, based on your assessment of the patient's motives, rationality, and immediate risk for suicide.

Some Comments for Therapists

Mental health professionals are similarly faced with a number of concerns related to assisted dying. If you are a therapist, you are charged with protecting the life of your client from her own wrongful actions. In working with a person who plans to end her life, it is therefore imperative that you feel absolutely comfortable with all aspects of her decision. In particular, you need to be certain of its rationality.

This responsibility is particularly pressing if the client has been referred to you specifically for counseling or assessment on the issue of assisted dying. Your active involvement in the decision process is then crucial, as the patient's physician may well be depending on your judgment. Because this can place an enormous burden on you, you need to carefully consider the precise nature of your role and your willingness to work with the client on this issue. If your role is merely to assess the rationality of the client, you must be absolutely comfortable that the end result of your work may be the client's assisted suicide. This dilemma is lessened if your role is to work therapeutically with the client on a range of issues.

Another concern pertains to the handling of confidentiality. Different considerations apply when you are seeing the patient alone, when you are seeing her jointly with her spouse, partner, or family, and when you are seeing all these individuals both singly and as a group. Family therapists often work exclusively with the entire group and discourage any private confidences that might create a special therapeutic relationship with one person. This restriction needs to be made clear to all participants at the onset of therapy.

Other therapists often see each partner or family member separately and treat any information received during a private session as confidential. They may encourage an individual to disclose any therapeutically relevant information to others in the larger group, but they will not insist on this. Still others adopt the more difficult position of maintaining the right to divulge any information they may have obtained from individual clients if they see a therapeutic benefit in doing so.

Should a terminally ill or incurable client inform you of her desire to die, your first task is to assess the risk of her following through, as well as the rationality of her thought process (which should not be confused with the rationality of the case for suicide in this instance). If you find your client to be rational and competent, your dilemma will be whether to require her to inform significant others of her desire to end her life or to divulge this information yourself. Given the extremely serious nature of the disclosure, it is generally preferable for the client to make it. But one way or another, significant relations need to be informed of your client's intentions, in as gentle a manner as possible. If these individuals are also receiving your counseling, then disclosure is mandatory.

Generally speaking, the ailing person should not end her life without giving someone close to her the opportunity to discuss the option she is considering and to share his thoughts and feelings about it. There are exceptions, however, as in the case of a long-term abusive relationship in which a client has been trapped for years and is now more imprisoned than ever because of her illness. But in such a case, a further question will have to be explored in your work with the client: Is her desire to die rooted solely in intolerable physical pain and suffering or in a hunger to escape the relationship? Only after you explore this latter issue with your client and know more about her relationship can you return to the question of disclosure. At that point you will have to decide whether anything can be gained by working to resolve the problems within the relationship or whether it is in the client's best interest to divulge her desire to die to her partner.

You might assume that the parties in a relationship would openly share life-and-death concerns as a matter of course, but several patients I have met have spoken of their fear of hurting their spouse or partner by discussing the issue of assisted suicide. They believed they would frighten the other if they were honest about their conflicting needs—on the one hand, to continue living for the sake of the partner, and on the other, to end their physical torment.

The topic of disclosure is often best broached with a client while working with her on issues related to her motivation for an assisted suicide, her concerns about the dying process and burdening others, her feelings about death, her desire for closure, any difficulties she may have communicating with others, her perceptions of the quality of her life and her relationships, and her fears about the effect of disclosure or the impact of her death on others. A therapeutic focus on such issues—say, her feelings about death—can be particularly important and help her gain a certain clarity about her own beliefs that she might be able to carry into discussions with her significant others. Similarly, her dialogue with you about her motivation for an assisted suicide can serve as a rehearsal for a similar discussion with her partner. In fact, you might ask your client to bring up these same topics with that person.

In a family counseling session, it is most important that the patient be able to express all her concerns and fears related to her illness and the dying process and to describe her quality of life as she experiences it. In some cases, it will be necessary to confront the fear of becoming a burden on others, which often figures in a patient's desire to die. Partners or other family members need to be given the opportunity to address that concern.

Such sessions may result in improved communication among the parties, regardless of whether they agree on assisted death. And they may also contribute to changes in the patient's feelings about her life. I have found that many—though certainly not all—initial firm decisions on assisted suicide gradually waver. Clinicians have a hand in this when they respond compassionately and pursue aggressive palliative care for previously unmet complaints. But equally influential are opportunities for the patient to communicate her concerns clearly and openly and to receive the love, support, and acceptance of her family. As a therapist, you can be especially helpful in providing occasions for such dialogue.

Should your client be unwilling to openly declare her desire to die, you will be faced with a moral and practical quandary. Ideally, others should be as prepared as possible for a person's death; unless absolutely necessary, it should not come as a surprise. At the very least, you should emphasize to your client the need to discharge any emotional responsibilities she may have toward others in her life and to give them opportunities to resolve any unfinished business. If the patient cannot accomplish this on her own, you might suggest group sessions with all parties to focus on these concerns.

Another point of importance is that, like other clinicians involved in assisted suicide, you face certain professional risks. If it can be proved that you were aware of your client's intentions but failed to intervene—or even to inform significant relations—you could be held negligent in this person's death.

Finally, it must be said that there may be times when a client presents goals that are neither appropriate nor desirable—indeed, that are detrimental to her best interests or to those of others. Assisted suicide may well fall into this category, particularly if the client has no intentions of sharing her thoughts or plans with a partner or other close family member. This reinforces the need to explore in therapy the client's underlying motives for wanting to die, any relationship issues that may exist, fears of abandonment, her perceptions about her significant relations, and the impact of her death or assisted suicide on others.

Where your client's goal is at odds with your professional values, you should examine closely the potential consequences of supporting it. If you conclude that you cannot endorse an assisted death, you should immediately either tell the client to seek another referral from her physician or offer to make such a referral yourself.

The following questions are designed to help you focus on the key issues involved in working with a client who is seeking an assisted death:

- What do you believe is the purpose of psychotherapy for a client with a life-threatening condition who is suffering intolerably and considering assisted suicide?

- Can you effectively work with such a client? Will you demand that this patient make a contract not to suicide during the course of assessment, counseling, and treatment? What if this person's suffering worsens?

- Do you see the purpose of individual therapy as helping the client to (1) better understand her motives; (2) see the possible effects of her actions on others; (3) achieve a sense of resolution with her own life and with others; (4) face the inevitability of her death; or (5) turn away from an assisted death and explore alternatives?

- What do you see as the purpose of conjoint or family therapy when one party is considering assisted suicide? Is it to help all clients obtain the tools to communicate more effectively among themselves? Is to help them achieve a sense of peace with their relationships, given the approach of death? Or is the purpose to achieve consensus on the decision for assisted suicide?

- What do you see as your responsibilities to an individual client who has expressed a desire to die?

- If such a client tells you the planned time and place of her assisted suicide, how would you deal with the issue of confidentiality?

- If your client tells you that she plans to disregard the opposition of her significant others and act on her own, would you keep this information confidential?

- What are your responsibilities to this person's significant others if they also are clients?

Emotional Risks

Before finally deciding to help your patient, you need to consider deeply how this action might affect you emotionally and in your professional dealings with other patients. Over the years, you may have worked with several patients as they proceeded through the dying process. You may have made numerous decisions with patients and families about withholding or withdrawing life-sustaining treatment. Nevertheless, you may view your participation in an assisted death differently, in part because of its questionable nature in both ethical and legal terms.

Performance of this action requires more than respect for the autonomous desire of your patient. It also demands your active involvement, your willingness to place the power of death in the hands of your patient, and your firm belief that the action is necessary for mercy.

To assess your likely emotional response to the assisted suicide you are being asked to participate in, you would do well to

- Reflect on your emotional responses to difficult deaths of former patients
- Remember what aspects of such deaths bothered you the most
- Ask yourself how these experiences may be influencing your current decision
- Consider all the aspects of this particular case and ponder how you might feel afterward
- Think how your involvement might affect your future relationships with other patients who have similar conditions, who make similar requests, or who are going through the dying process

As one clinician told me:

Turning down a request from a similar patient, and watching him die in a particularly brutal and unnecessary way, certainly influenced me the next time I was asked. . . . What that earlier death made me realize was my need to step back and let go of control, and accept that this was his desire, and his death, not mine.

Nevertheless, there was an emotional price to pay.

I have always felt this was the right thing to do. I have never had any doubts. But professionally, it was a very lonely experience. I didn't feel that I could bring it up with anyone. You really are in the closet with this stuff.

This isolation, which is also particularly common among family members who assist, has a broader dimension. Lacking the resources for full case consultation and the opportunity to receive assurance from peers that you indeed had no other choice, you could feel a sense of guilt or regret. Or you may have difficulty letting go of the experience. As another clinician told me:

I kept second-guessing myself, wondering if there wasn't something else I could've done. Like many doctors, I've never been good at relinquishing control to patients, especially around death. After all, we've been trained to believe that death is always the enemy. You're there to help them, you've got the expertise, and there's always another trick up your sleeve, or so you think. Now here comes a patient who says, "Death's not the problem, doc. Dying's the problem." I finally had to accept that I'd done my best, and this decision really was my patient's to make, and it was his life, and I was here to support him.

In the days following "Dr. Green's" involvement in the death of his patient, as described in the *Boston Globe* series, his feelings "ran wild." He was reported as saying, "I remember feeling electrified, and kind of astounded [by] the reality of it, that [my patient] had really done it, the finality of it, the sadness of it." He then added that he also was plagued by "feelings of guilt, worry I was going to get caught." There was no remorse, however. Instead, the act "marked a professional turning point." Previously opposed to assisted suicide, he said, "Part of this is how people change and see things differently." He commented that his patient and the situation persuaded him that his former position was wrong.

There is no way of knowing whether Green's reported transformation was just a device with which he could rationalize his actions. Perhaps. But I am convinced from my interviews with doctors and significant others who have assisted in suicide that whether the effects are positive or negative, and whether transformation is possible, depend on several factors: the overall quality and thoughtfulness of the decision process, the availability of opportunities for resolution of personal issues, the degree of acceptance the patient's decision has received from significant relations and the clinician, and the extent of untreatable suffering evident to those involved.

Those who have reflected with me on their involvement have described a range of responses and emotions. None of the clinicians ever saw an assisted death as something easy, as something that did not affect them in a profound way. As one physician told me:

> This is something I've done a half dozen times in twenty years. I now consider it necessary in extremely rare cases. It shouldn't come easy. If it does, something's wrong.

Another said:

> I've done this a few times, and while I've never doubted my actions, it doesn't mean that it didn't affect me. I don't like

being placed in this situation, where this is the only choice, but sometimes that's the nature of the work.

Or as yet another explained:

Current medical training focuses on putting feelings aside. You lose a patient, you forget about it and move on. We're trained to forget it and move on. This is a person who's been trained to look horror in the face and move on. But what really happens inside the doctor?

Questions to Ask Yourself

In short, you must be at peace with yourself when deciding to grant a patient's wish to hasten her final days. To that end, let us recap the questions that you must answer:

- Have I fully assessed all professional risks that might be involved in my helping this patient die, including the risk of arrest, prosecution, disciplinary action, and even the loss of my professional license?

- Have I fully considered how this action may affect me emotionally or in my professional dealings with other patients? Am I prepared to cope with a range of possible emotions?

- Have I taken fully into account the needs of my patient's significant relations and any potential opposition they have to her plans?

- Have I fully assessed the legal and emotional risks to the patient's significant others who themselves might become involved in her assisted suicide?

- Have I considered the possibility that a family member opposed to her plans might inform legal authorities?

- Have I thought about the possibility that my involvement might become known to strangers in the patient's circle of friends? Have I considered this risk and cautioned my patient not to discuss her plans for an assisted suicide or my potential involvement?

- Have I given thought to the issues surrounding confidentiality, especially if the patient has failed to inform significant relations of her plans? Have I fully emphasized the need for my patient to disclose her plans to other significant relations prior to my agreeing to help her die?

- Have I asked my patient to seek professional help to resolve any outstanding issues she may have with her significant relations?

- If I am part of a health care team, have I told my patient of my need to inform other members of the request? Have I informed other team members about the request? Have I sought their input? Have I informed them that I am considering the request?

- Have I considered the possibility of crisis intervention should it become apparent to me that the patient's decision is ill-advised and irrational and the risk of her suicide is high?

- Am I treating my decision to help her die as an extraordinary last resort in the face of increased intolerable suffering and the lack of effective treatment options?

***

What I have called for throughout this chapter is more intensive ways of communicating and responding to the concerns of your patient. I also have asked you to look closely at your own decision processes. This means questioning your own motives whenever possible and looking more deeply at the nature of your relationship with this specific individual. It also means examining the nature of the act itself. All of this is aimed at ensuring the highest quality of care as your patient moves through the illness and dying process.

This brings to mind the meaning of the term *euthanasia:* good death. We can learn much from this Greek word, though it has negative connotations to many. When you are considering whether or not to hasten a patient's death, I suggest that you ask yourself, "If I fulfilled this patient's request to die, would this be a good death?" and "Would this be the best way to care for my patient under the circumstances?" Finally, you need to ask, "Is there any other way I can work with my patient to ensure comfort in the weeks or months ahead, and even to increase the opportunity for a positive experience?"

I would argue that the likelihood of a positive experience and a good death can be enhanced if the patient's decision to die and your own thought processes about helping are framed within an established clinician-patient relationship of long duration. This promotes the development of a deeper understanding of your patient and all her needs. In this day of managed care, I recognize that such a relationship may not always be feasible. But if you and your patient do have a long-standing connection, I recommend that you take the effort to deepen it—and if you do not, do all that you can to create a substantive relationship on the basis of caring and compassion. And if you are part of a health care team, I urge you to encourage all team members to do the same, even as you focus on your individual tasks.

To the patient, a good death may be one in which both her own suffering and the emotional pain of her significant others are kept to a minimum. To members of her family, a good death may depend on their being able to fully accept her decision, recognizing the need for mercy and the appropriateness of the method and timing of her death. It will also be important that they experience a sense of resolution.

To some, a death cannot be good if it represents a life cut short. To others, method and timing are less important than alleviation of unnecessary suffering. Whether we have given much thought to it, each of us carries a personal ideal of the good death, which we see as a goal both for ourselves and for others. Encapsulating our deepest feelings about personal choice and letting go, this ideal dwells in our core.

Your responsibility as a clinician is to consult both your own idea of the good death and your patient's conception of it, and to do all in your power to satisfy the demands of each.

Until laws are changed, assisted dying will continue to be a secret act outside the accepted boundaries of medical practice. This means that whatever guidelines you work by will be those that you yourself have developed. I hope the discussion here and in the other chapters of this book will assist you in the achievement of that task.

Epilogue

The decision to help a patient to die is a decision to cross a special boundary. It redefines the nature of medical practice and the healer's role and radically alters the relationship between clinician and patient. Opponents of assisted suicide point to this as the reason to deny its availability. They claim that legalization or toleration of the procedure would transform physicians and nurses into killers, harden them against the value of human life, and destroy the trust on which the clinician-patient relationship rests.

This might indeed be true if assisted death were made available with few restrictions, meager guidelines for decision making, and no other choice for care. However, I am hopeful that it will never be easily available but will come to be seen as an option reserved for extraordinary cases. Then we may anticipate a more positive transformation than that predicted by opponents.

Such a model would enable clinicians to be increasingly willing to discuss the possibility of assisted suicide within the context of a variety of options. A practitioner's willingness to explore the issue would reflect a desire to meet the patient on new and compassionate ground, at the level of her physical and emotional suffering, and to lift responsibility and caring to a higher level. In this way, any final crossing of the boundary would first require expanding the healing role of clinicians and their approach to the care of terminally ill and incurable patients.

The availability of assisted suicide should not be seen as the ultimate answer to compassionate care, any more than the availability of hospice is. Both are social inventions that have come into being because of a perceived need by diverse groups for additional ways for people to face death.

The demand for assisted suicide, like the attention given to hospice, has grown out of increasing public discomfort with some of the newer powers of medicine and out of concern about the length and severity of the ordeal that dying often entails. In the 1950s, which witnessed the birth of what Albert Jonsen has termed the "age of rescue," an expanding range of technologies engendered a new sense in medicine that lives must be saved and prolonged whenever possible. Before long, this imperative became the standard of medical care. But as a consequence, less attention was paid to the whole patient, especially the person at the nexus between life and death, who could not necessarily be returned to a life of self-defined quality.

Although most of us would welcome the gift of a life reborn through medical achievements, we dread the prospect of a lingering and painful death for our family members or ourselves. Even health care professionals are concerned about these interventions. In her testimony before Congress, Kathleen Foley stated that four out of five physicians and nurses identified overtreatment as their major worry and that nearly two-thirds of attending physicians, and far more nurses, were concerned about inappropriate use of mechanical ventilation and cardiopulmonary resuscitation in terminal care. Conversely, nearly nine out of ten believed that in the area of pain control, undertreatment is the main problem. In other words, the public's worst fears about the dying process are often validated by health professionals themselves.

Where death used to be the only enemy, there is now another: the process of dying itself. The battle lines have therefore shifted, both for the public and for clinicians. Practical and ethical preoccupations, which formerly centered on such challenges as identifying appropriate recipients for dialysis or transplants and deciding whether to withhold or withdraw life-sustaining treatment, now focus increasingly on assisted suicide and euthanasia.

The first inklings of the rebellion against the "rescue model" could be seen as early as the mid–1960s, in the works of critics such as Elisabeth Kübler-Ross, who called attention to the denial of death within medical institutions and, as Christine Cassel and Bruce Vladeck put it, to "physicians' inability emotionally or clinically, to deal comfortably and competently with human mortality."

Open rebellion began ten years later when media attention focused on the case of Karen Ann Quinlan, who was hospitalized in a coma, placed on a ventilator, and diagnosed as being in a persistent vegetative state. Although Karen's parents requested removal of the ventilator, the hospital refused, fearing that such an action would violate the "do no harm" principle and expose the institution to tort liability. The New Jersey Supreme Court sided with the parents and argued that the case raised questions about traditional medical hegemony and paternalism. Thus ruling, the court intruded itself into the previously inviolable doctor-patient relationship.

This case struck a raw nerve. The image of a young woman being kept alive physiologically precipitated a wave of legislative initiatives to extend patient autonomy and the right to make advance decisions about the withholding or withdrawing of life-sustaining treatment. Within a year, legislation conferring a "right to die" was introduced in thirty-eight states, and within sixteen years, all fifty states recognized advance directives, whether in the form of living wills, medical powers of attorney, or other formal instructions for future care or surrogate decision-making.

More than a hundred other important cases followed during this period. In the 1983 *Barber* case, the California Court of Appeals ruled that physicians could not be held liable for discontinuing life support in medically futile situations and made no distinction between advanced life support and artificial nutrition and hydration. Further, in the *Cruzan* decision, the U.S. Supreme Court ruled that states could set reasonable standards for removal of artificial nutrition and hydration at the request of patients or their surrogates.

During these years, although true believers in the miracles of progress no doubt favored a model of care based on intervention and hope, an increasing number of dissenters began to express out-right terror at such a model. Their reaction, says Levinsky, seems to have been rooted in the "fear that doctors are determined to keep dehumanized bodies alive indefinitely, whatever the cost in human suffering."

By the early 1990s, following passage of the Patient Self-Determination Act, a new model of health care based on the right of patients to make autonomous medical decisions, and even to termi-nate life-sustaining care, had made substantial inroads on the rescue model, at least on paper. However, more recent studies show that pa-tients' wishes with respect to their health care are still often ignored.

The rebellion has led to two distinct developments, both of which focus on the concept of a "humane, compassionate, dignified death." One is the call for legalizing assisted suicide, and the other is hospice.

Hospice, which began in England in the 1960s with the work of Cicely Saunders, first came to America in 1974. It was con-sciously developed as an alternative to the rescue model, to meet the medical needs of patients—in their homes, whenever possi-ble—through pain control and symptom management. This model has stressed the emotional care of patients, which includes close, re-sponsive attention to their fears and affirmation of their values. The family unit is the preferred centerpiece of support.

In 1983, hospice became a reimbursable expense under Medi-care and has continued to grow. U.S. hospices now serve several hundred thousand persons at any one time, including more than 40 percent of all those dying from cancer and AIDS.

Although hospice provides a compassionate alternative to the rescue model, it does not go far enough for supporters of assisted sui-cide, who ask, "What of those who continue to suffer intolerably from various incurable or end-stage conditions, despite compre-hensive efforts to provide comfort?" They also ask, "What about those who are not in pain but are exhausted by the relentlessness of their physical infirmities and have little self-defined quality of life?" In a 1992 landmark article in the *New England Journal of Medicine*, Timothy Quill, Christine Cassel, and Diane Meier described such individuals. They ask us to consider "a former athlete, weighing 80 lb (36 kg) after an eight-year struggle with . . . [AIDS], who is losing his sight and his memory and is terrified of dementia" and "a writer with extensive bone metastases from lung cancer that has not responded to [treatment], who cannot accept the daily choice he must make between sedation and severe pain."

Such cases have prompted the rise of interest in assisted dying not so much by fear of intervention as by fears of unbearable suffering and the loss of dignity and autonomy. Even with hospice support, many people dread that the final dying process will be protracted, intolerable, and devastating to their quality of life. Like the growth of hospice, interest in assisted suicide has been a reaction against the rescue model and a reflection of deeper concerns many have about modern death. There is a feeling that it is not enough to withhold treatment; cases like those just described call for more radical action, as they seem to mock the potential for a dignified and peaceful death. Proponents see little dignity in relentless suffering from metastatic cancer or AIDS, or in the air hunger of constricted respiration.

Although its proponents see assisted death as the ultimate model of patient autonomy, critics ask whether this demand for control is a rejection of the rescue model or merely another version of it. The patient, they say, is still asking to be rescued—this time from the process of dying. Death is desired as an escape from possible future conditions, as well as from the experience of burdening others, the risk of abandonment, or the potential inadequacy of pain control. Some, like Kathleen Foley, claim that "requests for aid in dying fade with adequate pain control, psychological support, provision of family support, and with the promise that their symptoms would be controlled throughout the dying process." As I have argued throughout this book, there is much truth in this statement. But it doesn't tell the full story.

These criticisms ignore the fact that some people do die in objectionable ways, suffer intolerably, and see little point in being medicated to a natural end. Those who support assisted suicide say that ultimately it is a matter of personal choice, and that they have no interest in staying alive for the opportunities for profound wisdom and learning, reconciliation of relationships, and love that are promised by hospice proponents. Some, like Franklin Miller, also argue that in ignoring the need for mercy, critics are bolstering a paternalism that was once restricted to medical institutions and professionals but is now alive and well in the hospice model of death. As one man considering assisted suicide told me, "The problem with autonomy is that it enables us to live and die according to our own values and beliefs about our own best interests and to make mistakes." And so the debate goes on.

Despite the vehemence of the arguments against assisted suicide, I still expect to see a gradual breakdown in the presently firm opposition to it in the organized medical community. Patient requests for aid in dying are not rare, and as surveys show, the secret involvement of health care professionals is already widespread. In light of broad public support, it seems inevitable that the practice will be cautiously sanctioned in some manner within the next several years.

The reason is obvious, according to a 1996 article by David Orentlicher: "Such laws will once again bring society's legal rules in closer line with its moral values." Orentlicher points out that current laws and medical practice allow otherwise healthy individuals, such as a young woman hospitalized with asthma, to refuse temporary life-sustaining ventilation but deny the option of assisted suicide to patients near the ends of their lives who are suffering intolerably. Society's moral values would seem to demand the opposite. "The relevant difference is the context," he says, "not the act."

In whatever way such a change eventually takes place—through further court action, voter initiatives, legislation, or gradual changes in clinical practice guidelines—I would hope that it will require a cautious approach to decision making similar to what I have outlined in this book. I would also hope that it not come to pass in re-action against the continuing failure of clinicians to fully address the needs of dying patients, as I remain dubious of any approach that is built on the perceived failure of medicine.

So far the Supreme Court has upheld bans on assisted suicide but refused to rule out all bans in all circumstances, leaving the door open to further action by state legislatures or the initiative process. Oregon has already scheduled its referendum; others are likely else-where. New approaches will be tried, and the debate will continue.

I am troubled, however, by the changes that might result from the broad brush of the voter initiative. I have yet to see any initia-tive that treats assisted suicide as a rare and extraordinary option or that carries the potential for overall systematic change in the care of the dying.

I prefer the more restrictive and cautious approach that legisla-tion offers. Nevertheless, I am well aware of the gridlock that marks political life in this country, the lobbying efforts that influence elected officials, and the effect of negative campaigning by political opponents that often can quash enlightened debate and voter be-havior. Properly crafted legislation could allow for stringent controls and position assisted suicide in a framework that provides an ex-panded range of options and improvements, including wide-scale education in pain control, liberalization of drug policies, and addi-tional opportunities for palliative care efforts for the terminally and incurably ill in home, hospital, or other settings. The findings of the SUPPORT study show that the present quality of care for the dying in our medical institutions is unacceptable. I would have trouble supporting any legally proposed option for assisted suicide that fails to address these other issues.

In saying this, I am not suggesting that implementation of this practice must wait for a perfect system of health care to be in place; that is certainly not foreseeable within the next several decades, if ever. And that demand ignores the fact that physician-assisted sui-cide will continue to be practiced by clinicians, as it is now, secretly and outside the law. Knowing this, I would hope that professional medical societies and institutions begin to provide practitioners with clinical guidelines to help them respond to patients' requests and make appropriate referrals and decisions. To ignore doing so places too great a burden on clinicians and their suffering patients. By leaving clinicians alone to reinvent the wheel with every request, it also increases the risk of inappropriate responses.

Given the potential for the eventual implementation of physician aid in dying in some locale, I would, ideally, like to see the practice linked to a number of major initiatives for change. The first would be to improve the quality of pain control—and the quality of life—for patients wherever they reside. In addition to improved education in pain control, physicians and nursing professionals need further instruction in the philosophy behind palliative care. Similarly, national and state drug policies require serious rethinking. To date, federal and state drug laws and DEA regulations have done little to solve problems of abuse but have clearly been detrimental to patients in need of relief.

Certain other issues should also be addressed, as they may be contributing factors in a patient's desire to die. One of these is the quality of nursing care for the dying. Good nursing care goes hand in hand with effective treatment for pain and suffering. It can greatly reduce the emotional and practical stress on families of the dying, and by so doing may help to allay patients' concerns about burdening their caregivers. Expansion of the availability of home and residential hospice programs is key here, as is increased respite for caregivers and palliative care within hospital settings.

One of the brakes on hospice expansion is current Medicare reimbursement guidelines, which penalize hospices that serve patients for more than a specified number of days. Although the average hospice patient is admitted some thirty-six days before death, there are others who "outlive" hospice by several months. This should be seen as a benefit rather than a deficit, especially given the high-cost alternative of revolving-door admissions to hospitals.

A closely related issue is the necessity for earlier hospice referral. Several factors are involved here, ranging from problems of prognosis to the difficulty many clinicians have in declaring that a patient is terminal. Years of medical training and a persistent belief in the rescue model play a significant role. It is also exceedingly difficult psychologically for clinicians to inform patients that their conditions are beyond hope. One solution is continuing education to reduce the influence of the rescue model in health care decisions near the end of life. Another is the creation of new models of care that might reside somewhere between the rescue and hospice models.

On a brighter front, there is some positive movement in the area of hospice coverage. Some programs are expanding their categories of care to include patients whom they may not have seen in the past, including those with heart disease, lung disease, and Alzheimer's. Such patients will now be able stay at home, no longer subject to hospitalization except in the most severe circumstances. Moreover, we are likely to see palliative programs for a range of diagnoses.

As regards hospital care for the dying, another hopeful sign is the approval by the Health Care Financing Administration (HCFA) of a diagnostic code for palliative care. This enables coders who review hospital charts to indicate that palliative care was provided to a dying patient. HCFA analysts will now be able to study the feasibility of creating a special diagnostic-related group (DRG), which would allow payment for such care, as well as the care of other patients who die while hospitalized.

Another problem area is institutional care. The fear of institutionalization remains a significant factor in many patients' consideration of an assisted death. The heart of the problem is the loss of freedom that care in a skilled nursing facility may represent. This negative image is due in part to the emotional distance that is perceived to be created between the dying and the living, and in particular between patients and their families. This does not have to continue.

Currently, several innovative models are being looked at. Moreover, with the continued aging of the population, we are likely to see new types of skilled nursing facilities and radically different models for housing and caregiving, including shared living arrangements with hospice patients and others. We have yet to scratch the surface. But innovation is needed sooner rather than later. It should include an increase in the availability and types of residential hospices and changes in the nature of extended care facilities. Public fear of institutionalization can be alleviated only by changing the nature of the institutional experience.

An unknown ingredient in all of this is managed care. Some observers suggest that one benefit of managed care may well be further expansion of palliative medicine for the dying, if only for the purpose of saving costs. As a hospice medical director recently told me:

> What was standing in the way was fee-for-service medicine, because doctors didn't have any impetus to stop doing everything to everybody. With Medicare becoming managed Medicare, suddenly you have physicians who are begging to come up with new ways for caring for these people at home.

For good or ill, some people believe that financial incentives may ultimately be the key to institutional change in the care of the dying. Perhaps, but I remain hesitant to embrace any model based on profit and loss. Rather than providing substantive treatment, such a model could lead us down a slippery slope of health care rationing to the denial of care for persons with life-threatening conditions and enforced palliative care for the dying or for other patients considered economically untreatable.

Critics of assisted suicide have recently taken to arguing that managed care and the "right to die" are incompatible because of the financial incentives to bring costly treatments and hospitalization to an end. They argue that the practice, if made available, would fall into the hands of the unscrupulous and would pave the way for a harsh transformation of medicine. For example, Daniel Callahan, in a 1996 article, observed: "One's ear does not have to be very close to the ground to hear it said that legalizing physician-assisted suicide could help hold down the costs of health care for the elderly."

There are real concerns about managed care, but the primary worry is for those needing expensive procedures, not palliative care at the end of life. As Orentlicher stated in his 1996 article:

> We cannot distinguish assisted suicide in terms of these concerns. Indeed, finances are more problematic with the withdrawal of treatment, because the patient dependent on a ventilator or dialysis is generating higher health care costs than the terminally ill patient who is not dependent on life-sustaining treatment.

Callahan's argument against assisted suicide, based on economic incentives, further assumes that current models of managed care will remain in place. That is highly unlikely. In fact, these very fears are fueling some of the current backlash against health maintenance organizations (HMOs) and for-profit managed care organizations (MCOs).

The severe scrutiny is certain to continue. Ginzberg and Ostow claim that the era of managed care is coming to an end. They suggest that more public outcries about this model of "health care delivery" will inevitably lead to further government regulation of policies and practices. Jerome Kassirer remains doubtful of such a demise but believes that they

> will have to show that they have become better citizens: that they care about more than profits, that they do not skimp on care, that they support their just share of . . . the care of the poor, that they no longer muzzle physicians, and that they can offer something special.

Another issue, unlikely to be addressed anytime soon, is that of universal access to health care, which is still a distant vision. At the present time, there are more than forty million Americans who are without even minimum coverage. Many postpone diagnosis and treatment for any but the most severe symptoms, increasing the potential that treatable conditions will become life-threatening. Further, without coverage, the care these people do receive carries the risk of sending them or their families into poverty.

It is in the middle of this fray that the call for assisted suicide has been raised. Despite all of these apparent problems, however, I remain hopeful for the future of patient care. I am certain that the care of the dying will improve, and I hope that when assisted suicide is eventually permitted as a rare option, the practice will not bring up images of Nazi Germany. I see no road to murder. On the contrary. If anything has come out of this debate, it has been the greatly expanded interest in hospice and knowledge of the present inadequacy of pain control measures. This is a benefit. And even the rise of managed care, decried by so many as a sign of the diminishment of quality, carries the potential for turning medicine to new directions, even if through rebellion. Together, all of these developments, including assisted suicide, have led to the increasing recognition that the process of dying needs to be treated differently.

Institutional change cannot remove the motives for assisted death in all cases, but better overall care might redirect some of those at the outer perimeter of this decision. In saying this, I do not mean to step so heavily on the liberty interest of patients. My task is not to keep alive against their will those who are suffering intolerably. Nor is yours. Rather, we must work toward opening a full range of paths, for it is only in this way that freedom of choice can be upheld. As Kay Holt has said:

> Fixed rigid opinions about whether it is right or wrong to assist our patients in alleviating suffering are of little value. Until we can rationally and thoroughly discuss all options as possible solutions in certain situations, the division of opinion will continue to obstruct good patient care in the truest sense of

the word. There is no single opinion or solution that is applicable to every patient. The simple, but often overlooked, truth is that every patient is different and each circumstance requires the responsible physician to carefully consider all factors present.

Innovation breeds innovation, albeit often by a Hegelian dialectic, and the call for assisted suicide may lead to yet other turning points and advances in care. My hope derives from my faith in health practitioners, most of whom, I am certain, selected their career paths out of a desire to heal, or at least to care.

The medical imperative born in the age of rescue has been under serious attack. It has been wounded, since *Quinlan*, by the movements for patients' rights and the right to die. And it has been wounded further by increased health care costs and the move toward managed care. One may rejoice that these are not grave wounds, because underlying the rescue model is a positive force both to heal and to care. Instead of craving its demise, I look forward to its redefinition, where its long-standing emphasis on curing can be balanced by acceptance of the power of caring, and acknowledgment of both the desires of patients and a fact of life called death. We all must die—as one clinician put it, "We are all pregnant with death. It may be made cleaner, easier, quicker, or less physically painful, but it will not go away." Neither will the call for assisted suicide or the dilemmas for medicine and therapy that it may pose. As a clinician, your task is to know this and to understand the consequences for your patient and yourself.

No matter how involved you are professionally in the larger issues facing medicine, they ultimately take on a different character as you care for your patients and attempt to cure their ills and alleviate their suffering. This relationship is primary. Nevertheless, it is here where the issues surrounding patient autonomy, the limits of mercy, the options for treatment, and your response to requests for aid in dying become real. It is here where your own professional

skills and ethical beliefs are put to the test. As David Loxterkamp
has stated:

> We are obliged to listen to licensing boards, credentialing
> committees, peer-review organizations, and insurance carriers.
> But they do not define us. The one person who will challenge
> us the most, who will deliver us to our finest hours, who will
> talk us through every moral conundrum, is the patient, who
> we thought needed *us*.

References

Alpers, A., & Lo, B. (1995). Physician-assisted suicide in Oregon: A bold experiment. *Journal of the American Medical Association, 274,* 483–87.

American Psychiatric Association. (1994). *Diagnostic and statistical manual of mental disorders* (4th ed.). Washington, DC: American Psychiatric Association.

Amundsen, D. W. (1978). The physician's obligation to prolong life: A medical duty without classical roots. *Hastings Center Report, 8,* 4, 23–31.

Angell, M. (1997). The Supreme Court and physician-assisted suicide: The ultimate right [Editorial]. *New England Journal of Medicine, 336,* 50–53.

Annas, G. J. (1994). Death by prescription: The Oregon Initiative. *New England Journal of Medicine, 331,* 1240–43.

Annas, G. J. (1995). How we lie. *Hastings Center Report, 25,* 6, 12–14.

Annas, G. J., & Densberger, J. E. (1984). Competence to refuse medical treatment: Autonomy versus paternalism. *University of Toledo Law Review, 15,* 561–96.

Annas, G. J. (1996). The promised end: Constitutional aspects of physician-assisted suicide. *New England Journal of Medicine, 335,* 683–87.

Aroskar, M. A. (1994). Nursing and the euthanasia debate. *Journal of Professional Nursing, 10,* 5.

Asch, D. (1996). The role of critical care nurses in euthanasia and assisted suicide. *New England Journal of Medicine, 334,* 1374–79.

Bachman, J. G., Alcser, K. H., Doukas, D. J., Lichtenstein, R. L., Corning, A. D., & Brody, H. (1996). Attitudes of Michigan physicians and the public toward legalizing physician-assisted suicide and voluntary euthanasia. *New England Journal of Medicine, 334,* 303–9.

Back, A. L., Wallace, J. I., Starks, H. E., & Pearlman, R. A. (1996). Physician assisted suicide and euthanasia in Washington State: Patient requests and physician responses. *Journal of the American Medical Association, 275,* 919–25.

Barber v. Superior Court, 195 Cal. Rptr. 4848 (Ct. App. 1983).

Baron, C. H., Bergstresser, C., Brock, D. W., Cole, G. F., Dorfman, N. S., Johnson, J. A., Schnipper, L. E., Vorenberg, J., & Wanzer, S. H. (1996). A model state act to authorize and regulate physician-assisted suicide. *Harvard Journal on Legislation, 33,* 1.

Barry, R. L. (1994). *Breaking the thread of life: On rational suicide.* New Brunswick, NJ: Transaction.

Battin, M. P. (1994). *The least worst death: Essays in bioethics at the end of life.* New York: Oxford University Press.

Battin, M. P. (1995). *Ethical issues in suicide.* Upper Saddle River, NJ: Prentice Hall.

Baume, P., & O'Malley, E. (1994). Euthanasia: Attitudes and practices of medical practitioners. *Medical Journal of Australia, 161,* 137–64.

Bay Area Network of Ethics Committees. (1997). *BANEC-generated guidelines for comprehensive care of the terminally ill.* Bay Area Network of Ethics Committees.

Beauchamp, T. L., & Childress, J. F. (1989). *Principles of biomedical ethics* (3rd ed.). New York: Oxford University Press.

Benrubi, G. I. (1992). Euthanasia: The need for procedural safeguards. *New England Journal of Medicine, 326,* 197–99.

Blendon, R. J., Szalay, U. S., & Knox, R. A. (1992). Should physicians aid their patients in dying? The public perspective. *Journal of the American Medical Association, 267,* 2658–62.

Bodenheimer, T. (1996). The HMO backlash: Righteous or reactionary? *New England Journal of Medicine, 335,* 1601–4.

Bonger, B. (1991). *The suicidal patient: Clinical and legal standards of care.* Washington, DC: American Psychological Association.

Breitbart, W., Rosenfeld, B. D., & Passil, S. D. (1996). Interest in physician-assisted suicide among ambulatory HIV-infected patients. *American Journal of Psychiatry, 153,* 2237–42.

Brock, D. W. (1992). Voluntary active euthanasia. *Hastings Center Report, 22,* 10–22.

Brody, H. (1992). Assisted death: A compassionate response to a medical failure. *New England Journal of Medicine, 327,* 1384–88.

Brody, H. (1992). *The healer's power.* New Haven, CT: Yale University Press.

Brody, H. (1996). Attitudes of Michigan physicians and the public toward legalizing physician-assisted suicide and voluntary euthanasia. *New England Journal of Medicine, 334,* 303–9.

Brown, J. H., Henteleff, P., Baracat, S., & Rowe, C. J. (1986). Is it normal for terminally ill patients to desire death? *American Journal of Psychiatry, 143,* 208–11.

Byock, I. R. (1993). The euthanasia/assisted suicide debate matures. *American Journal of Hospice and Palliative Care, 10,* 8–11.

Byock, I. R. (1997). *Dying well: The prospect for growth at the end of life.* New York: Riverhead.

Callahan, D. (1987). *Setting limits: Medical goals in an aging society.* New York: Simon & Schuster.

Callahan, D. (1990). *What kind of life? The limits of medical progress.* New York: Simon & Schuster.

Callahan, D. (1992). When self-determination runs amok. *Hastings Center Report, 22,* 52–55.

Callahan, D. (1996). Controlling the costs of health care for the elderly: Fair means and foul. *New England Journal of Medicine, 335,* 744–46.

Campbell, C. S., Hare, J., & Matthews, P. (1995). Conflicts of conscience: Hospice and assisted suicide. *Hastings Center Report, 25,* 3, 36–43.

Cassel, C. K., & Meier, D. E. (1990). Morals and moralism in the debate over euthanasia and assisted suicide. *New England Journal of Medicine, 323,* 750–52.

Cassel, C. K., & Vladeck, B. C. (1996). ICD–9 code for palliative or terminal care. *New England Journal of Medicine, 335,* 1232–34.

Chochinov, H. M., Wilson, K. G., Enns, M., et al. (1995). Desire for death in the terminally ill. *American Journal of Psychiatry, 152,* 1185–91.

Ciesielski-Carlucci, C. (1993). Physician attitudes and experiences with assisted suicide: Results of a small opinion survey. *Cambridge Quarterly of Healthcare Ethics, 2,* 39–44.

Cohen, J. S., Fihn, S. D., Boyko, E. J., Jonsen, A. R., & Wood, R. W. (1994). Attitudes toward assisted suicide and euthanasia among physicians in Washington State. *New England Journal of Medicine, 331,* 89–94.

Colt, G. (1991). *The enigma of suicide*. New York: Simon & Schuster.

Compassion in Dying v. *Washington*, 79 F. 3d 790 (9th Cir. 1996).

Conwell, Y. (1994). Physician-assisted suicide: A mental health perspective. *Suicide and Life-Threatening Behavior*, 24, 326–33.

Conwell, Y., & Caine, E. D. (1991). Rational suicide and the right to die: Reality and myth. *New England Journal of Medicine*, 325, 1100.

Cotten, P. (1993). Rational suicide: No longer "crazy"? *Journal of the American Medical Association*, 270, 797.

Cotten, P. (1993). Talk to people about dying—they can handle it, say geriatricians and patients. *Journal of the American Medical Association*, 269, 321–22.

Council on Ethical and Judicial Affairs, American Medical Association. (1992). Decisions near the end of life. *Journal of the American Medical Association*, 267, 2229–33.

Council on Ethical and Judicial Affairs, American Medical Association. (1994). Physician-assisted suicide. *Issues in Law and Medicine*, 10, 91–97.

Cruzan v. *Director, Missouri Department of Health*. (1990). 497 U.S. 261, 110 S. Ct. 284.

Curtin, L. L. (1995). Nurses take a stand on assisted suicide. *Nursing Management*, 26, 71–76.

Death with Dignity Act. (1995). 1995 Oregon Laws Ch.3 (Initiative measure no. 16).

Dworkin, R. (1993). *Life's dominion: An argument about abortion, euthanasia, and individual freedom*. New York: Knopf.

Dworkin, R., Nagel, T., Nozick, R., Rawls, J., Scanlon, T., & Thomson, J. J. (1997). Assisted suicide: The philosophers' brief. *New York Review of Books*, 64, 7, 41–47.

Emmanuel, E. J. (1994). Euthanasia: Historical, ethical, and empirical perspectives. *Archives of Internal Medicine*, 154, 1890–1901.

Engelhardt, H. T., Jr. (1986). *The foundations of bioethics*. New York: Oxford University Press.

Engelhardt, H. T., Jr. (1989). Death by free choice: Modern variations on an antique theme. In B. A. Brody (Ed.), *Suicide and euthanasia: Historical and contemporary themes*. Norwell, MA: Kluwer.

Fins, J. J., & Bacchetta, M. D. (1994). The physician-assisted suicide and euthanasia debate: An annotated bibliography of representative articles. *Journal of Clinical Ethics*, 5, 329–40.

Fletcher, J. (1954). *Morals and medicine*. Boston: Beacon Press.

Foley, K. A. (1995). The treatment of cancer pain. *New England Journal of Medicine, 313*, 85.

Foley, K. A. (1996, April 29). Medical issues related to physician-assisted suicide. Testimony before the House Judiciary Subcommittee on the Constitution, Washington, DC.

Foley, K. A. (1996). The relationship of pain and symptom management to patient requests for physician-assisted suicide. *Journal of Pain and Symptom Management, 6*, 289–97.

Foley, K. A. (1997). Competent care for the dying instead of physician-assisted suicide [Editorial]. *New England Journal of Medicine, 336*, 54–58.

Gaylin, W., Kass, L. R., Pellegrino, E. D., & Siegler, M. (1988). Doctors must not kill. *Journal of the American Medical Association, 259*, 2139–40.

Ginzberg, E., & Ostow, M. (1997). Managed care: A look back and a look ahead. *New England Journal of Medicine, 336*, 1018–20.

Glick, S. M. (1997). Unlimited human autonomy: A cultural bias? *New England Journal of Medicine, 336*, 954–56.

Hardwig, J. (1990). What about the family? *Hastings Center Report, 20*, 2, 5–10.

Heckler, R. A. (1994). *Waking up alive: The descent, the attempt and the return to life after suicide*. New York: Putnam.

Heilig, S., & Jamison, S. (1996). Physician aid-in-dying: Toward a harm reduction approach. *Cambridge Quarterly of Healthcare Ethics, 5*, 113–20.

Hendin, H. (1982). *Suicide in America*. New York: Norton.

Hendin, H. (1995). Selling death and dignity. *Hastings Center Report, 25*, 3, 19–23.

Holt, K. G. (1994). Letter [on Quill, 1993]. *Journal of the American Medical Association, 271*, 23.

Humphry, D. (1993). *Final exit*. New York: Dell.

In re Quinlan, 335 A.2d 647 (N.J. 1976).

It's over, Debbie. (1988). *Journal of the American Medical Association, 259*, 272.

Jamison, S. (1996). *Final acts of love: Families, friends, and assisted dying*. New York: Tarcher/Putnam.

Jamison, S. (1996). When drugs fail: Assisted deaths and not-so-lethal drugs. *Journal of Pain and Symptom Management, 4*, 223–43.

Johanson, G. (1994). *Physician's handbook of symptom relief in terminal care*. Santa Rosa, CA: Sonoma County Academic Foundation for Excellence.

Jonsen, A. R. (1993). To help the dying die: A new duty for anesthesiologists? *Anesthesiology, 78*, 225–228.

Jonsen, A. R., Siegler, M., & Winslade, W. J. (1992). *Clinical ethics* (rev. ed.). New York: Macmillan.

Kamisar, Y. (1993). Are laws against assisted suicide unconstitutional? *Hastings Center Report, 23*, 3, 32–41.

Kass, L. R. (1989). Neither for love nor money: Why doctors must not kill. *Public Interest, 94*, 25–46.

Kass, L. R. (1992). "I will give no deadly drug": Why doctors must not kill. *American College of Surgeons Bulletin, 77*, 3, 6–17.

Kassirer, J. P. (1997). Is managed care here to stay? *New England Journal of Medicine, 336*, 14, 1013–14.

Koenig, H. G. (1993). Legalizing physician-assisted suicide: Some thoughts and concerns. *Journal of Family Practice, 37*, 171–79.

Kübler-Ross, E. (1969). *On death and dying*. Old Tappan, NJ: Macmillan.

Kuhse, H., & Singer, P. (1988). Doctors' practices and attitudes regarding voluntary euthanasia. *Medical Journal of Australia, 148*, 623–27.

Kuhse, H., & Singer, P. (1993). Voluntary euthanasia and the nurse: An Australian survey. *International Journal of Nursing Studies, 30*, 311–22.

Lee, M. A., Nelden, H. D., Tilden, V. P., Ganzini, L., Schmidt, T. A., & Tolle, S. W. (1996). Legalizing assisted suicide: Views of physicians in Oregon. *New England Journal of Medicine, 334*, 310–15.

Lehr, D. E. (1993, April 25–27). Death and the doctor's hand. *Boston Globe*.

Levinsky, N. G. (1996). The purpose of advance medical planning: Autonomy for patients or limitation of care? *New England Journal of Medicine, 335*, 741–43.

Lewin, T. (1996, March 8). Ruling sharpens assisted-suicide debate. *New York Times*, p. A14.

Lifton, R. J. (1986). *Nazi doctors: Medical killing and the psychology of genocide*. New York: Basic Books.

Loewy, E. H. (1992). Healing and killing, harming and not harming: Physician participation in euthanasia and capital punishment. *Journal of Clinical Ethics, 3*, 29–34.

Loxterkamp, D. (1996). Hearing voices: How should doctors respond to their calling? *New England Journal of Medicine, 335,* 1991–93.

Lynn, J. (1996). Caring at the end of our lives. *New England Journal of Medicine, 335,* 201–2.

Maltsberger, J. T. (1986). *Suicide risk: The formulation of clinical judgment.* New York: NYU Press.

Maris, R., Berman, A. L., Maltsberger, J. T., & Yufit, R. (Eds.). *Assessment and prediction of suicide.* New York: Guilford Press.

Marzuk, P. M. (1994). Suicide and terminal illness. *Death Studies, 18,* 497–512.

Mayo, D. (1993, Spring). Rational suicide revisited: Can we find a common ground? *Newslink,* pp. 6–7.

Miles, S. H. (1994). Physicians and their patients' suicides. *Journal of the American Medical Association, 271,* 1786–88.

Miller, F. G. (1995). The good death, virtue, and physician-assisted death: An examination of the hospice way of death. *Cambridge Quarterly of Healthcare Ethics, 4,* 92–97.

Miller, F. G., & Brody, H. (1995). Professional integrity and physician-assisted death. *Hastings Center Report, 25,* 3, 8–17.

Miller, F. G., & Fins, J. J. (1996). A proposal to restructure hospital care for dying patients. *New England Journal of Medicine, 334,* 1740–42.

Miller, F. G., Quill, T. E., Brody, H., Fletcher, J. C., Gostin, L. O., & Meier, D. E. (1994). Regulating physician-assisted death. *New England Journal of Medicine, 331,* 119–23.

Mor, V., Greer, D. S., & Kastenbaum, R. (1988). *The hospice experiment.* Baltimore: John Hopkins University Press.

National Association of Social Workers. (1994). Client self-determination in end-of-life decisions. In *Social work speaks: NASW policy statements* (3rd ed.)(pp. 58–61). Washington, DC: NASW Press.

Nelson, J. L. (1992). Taking families seriously. *Hastings Center Report, 22,* 4, 6–12.

Nuland, S. B. (1994). *How we die: Reflections on life's final chapter.* New York: Knopf.

Omnibus Reconciliation Act of 1990, Public Law No. 100–508, Sections 4206, 4751, 104 Stat. 1388 (1990, November 5).

Orentlicher, D. (1989). Physician participation in assisted suicide. *Journal of the American Medical Association, 262,* 1844–45.

Orentlicher, D. (1996). The legalization of physician-assisted suicide. *New England Journal of Medicine, 335*, 663–67.

Osgood, N. J., & Eisenhandler, S. A. (1994). Gender and assisted and acquiescent suicide: A suicidologist's perspective. *Issues in Law and Medicine, 9*, 361–74.

Peck, M. S. (1997). *Denial of the soul: Spiritual and medical perspectives on euthanasia and mortality.* New York: Harmony Books.

Pellegrino, E. D. (1992). Doctors must not kill. *Journal of Clinical Ethics, 3*, 95–102.

Quill v. Vacco, 80 F.3d 716 (2d Cir. 1996).

Quill, T. E. (1991). Death and dignity: A case of individualized decision making. *New England Journal of Medicine, 324*, 691–94.

Quill, T. E. (1993). *Death and dignity: Making choices and taking charge.* New York: Norton.

Quill, T. E. (1993). Doctor, I want to die. Will you help me? *Journal of the American Medical Association, 270*, 870–73.

Quill, T. E. (1994). Physician-assisted death: Progress or peril? *Suicide and Life-Threatening Behavior, 24*, 315–25.

Quill, T. E., Cassel, C. K., & Meier, D. E. (1992). Care of the hopelessly ill: Proposed clinical criteria for physician-assisted suicide. *New England Journal of Medicine, 327*, 1380–84.

Rachels, J. (1975). Active and passive euthanasia. *New England Journal of Medicine, 292*, 78–80.

Rachels, J. (1986). *The end of life: Euthanasia and mortality.* New York: Oxford University Press.

Raffin, T. (1991, March 15). Withholding and withdrawing life support. *Hospital Practice,* pp. 133–55.

Reigle, J. (1995). Should the patient decide when to die? *RN, 58*, 57–61.

Rooijmans, H. G., Doukas, D. J., Waterhouse, D., Gorenflo, D. W., & Seid, J. (1995). Attitudes and behaviors on physician-assisted death: A study of Michigan oncologists. *Journal of Clinical Oncology, 13*, 1055–61.

Rothman, D. J. (1991). *Strangers at the bedside.* New York: Basic Books.

Rousseau, P. (1992). Why give IV fluids to the dying? *Patient Care, 26*, 12, 71–74.

Rousseau, P. (1996). Terminal sedation in the care of dying patients. *Archives of Internal Medicine, 156*, 1785.

Roy, D. J. (1993). When the dying demand death [Editorial]. *Journal of Palliative Care, 9*, 3–4.

Rupp, M. T., & Isenhower, H. L. (1994). Pharmacists' attitudes toward physician-assisted suicide. *American Journal of Hospital Pharmacy, 51*, 69–74.

Scanlon, C. (1995). Euthanasia and nursing practice: Right question, wrong answer. *New England Journal of Medicine, 334*, 1401–2.

Shavelson, L. (1995). *A chosen death: The dying confront assisted suicide.* New York: Simon & Schuster.

Shneidman, E. S. (1992). Rational suicide and psychiatric disorders. *New England Journal of Medicine, 326*, 889–90.

Shneidman, E. S. (1993). *Suicide as psychache: A clinical approach to self-destructive behavior.* Northvale, NJ: Aronson.

Singer, P. (1994). *Rethinking life and death: The collapse of our traditional ethics.* New York: St. Martin's Press.

Singer, P., & Siegler, M. (1990). Euthanasia: A critique. *New England Journal of Medicine, 322*, 1881–83.

Slome, L. R., Mitchell, T. F., Charlebois, E., Benevedes, J. M., & Abrams, D. I. (1997). Physician-assisted suicide and patients with human immunodeficiency virus disease. *New England Journal of Medicine, 336*, 417–20.

SUPPORT Team Principal Investigators. (1995). A controlled trial to improve care for seriously ill hospitalized patients. *Journal of the American Medical Association, 274*, 1591–98.

Vacco v. Quill, No. 95–1858 (1997).

Vachon, M. L. S. (1987). *Occupational stress in the care of the critically ill, the dying, and the bereaved.* New York: Hemisphere.

van Delden, J. J. M., Pijnenborg, L., & van der Maas, P. J. (1993). The Remmelink study: Two years later. *Hastings Center Report, 23*, 6–24.

van der Maas, P. J., van Delden, J. J. M., & Pijnenborg, L. (1992). *Euthanasia and other medical decisions concerning the end of life: An investigation performed upon request of the commission of inquiry into the medical practice concerning euthanasia.* Health Policy Monographs, Vol. 2. Amsterdam: Elsevier.

van der Maas, P. J., van Delden, J. J. M., Pijnenborg, L., & Looman, C. W. N. (1991). Euthanasia and other medical decisions concerning the end of life. *Lancet, 338*, 669–74.

van der Maas, P. J., van der Wal, G., Haverkate, I., et al. (1996). Euthanasia, physician-assisted suicide, and other medical practices involving the end of life in the Netherlands, 1990–95. *New England Journal of Medicine, 335,* 1699–1705.

Ventafridda, V. (1987). Therapeutic strategy. In M. Swerdlow & V. Ventafridda (Eds.), *Cancer pain.* Lancaster, England: MTV Press.

Walter, J. J., & Shannon, T. A. (Eds.). (1990). *Quality of life: The new medical dilemma.* Mahwah, NJ: Paulist Press.

Wanzer, S. H., Adelstein, J., Cranford, R. E., et al. (1984). The physician's responsibility toward hopelessly ill patients. *New England Journal of Medicine, 310,* 955–59.

Wanzer, S. H., Federman, D. D., Adelstein, J., Cassel, C. K., Cassem, E., Cranford, R. E., Hook, E. W., Lo, B., Moertel, C. G., Safar, P., Stone, A., & van Eys, J. (1989). The physician's responsibility toward hopelessly ill patients: A second look. *New England Journal of Medicine, 320,* 844–49.

Ward, B. J., & Tate, P. A. (1994). Attitudes among NHS doctors to requests for euthanasia. *British Medical Journal, 308,* 1332–34.

Washington v. Quill, No. 96–110 (1997).

Werth, J. L., Jr. (1996). *Rational suicide? Implications for mental health professionals.* Washington, DC: Taylor & Francis.

Werth, J. L., Jr., & Cobia, D. C. (1995). Empirically based criteria for rational suicide: A survey of psychotherapists. *Suicide and Life-Threatening Behavior, 25,* 231–240.

Werth, J. L., Jr., & Liddle, B. J. (1994). Psychotherapists' attitudes toward suicide. *Psychotherapy: Theory, Research and Practice, 31,* 440–48.

Winokur, G., & Black, D. W. (1992). Suicide: What can be done? *New England Journal of Medicine, 327,* 490–91.

World Health Organization. (1996). *Cancer pain relief* (2nd ed.). Geneva, Switzerland: World Health Organization.

About the Author

Stephen Jamison, a social psychologist and ethicist, is an adjunct faculty member in the Department of Social and Behavioral Sciences at the University of California, San Francisco. He also directs Life and Death Consultations, a consultancy service in Mill Valley, working with health care professionals and families on communication issues at the end of life. He is currently involved in research on alternative models of caregiving.

Jamison obtained his Ph.D. in 1986 from the University of California, Davis, where he taught courses in death and dying and family studies for several years. He is a former regional director of the Hemlock Society U.S.A. and has also served as president of the Mental Health Association of Marin County. He is the author of *Final Acts of Love: Families, Friends, and Assisted Dying* (1996).

Index

G

Ginzberg, E., 229
Good death, notion of, 25–26, 217
Great Britain, 21, 202, 222

H

Hastening death: and cessation of food and
    water, 163–164; and double effect,
    162–163; and removal of life-sustaining
    treatment, 163; and sedation to coma,
    164; versus assisted dying, 165–167
Healing role, expansion of, 219–232
Health Care Financing Administration
    (HCFA), 227
Heckler, R. A., 100
Hegel, G.F.W., 231
Hemlock Society U.S.A., 3
Hendin, H., 41
Hippocratic Oath, 20
Holt, K. G., 230–231
Homemade assisted death, 187
Hopelessness, 99–103. See also Depression;
    Despair
Hospice: as alternative to rescue model of
    treatment, 222; benefits of, 161–162,
    and concerns over newer powers of
    medicine, 220; limits of, 28–30; and
    Medicare, 226; and process of dying, 25;
    psychospiritual work of, 173; and termi-
    nal sedation, 165, 166
"How to" manuals, 6, 54
Humphry, D., 54, 190

I

Impulsivity, risk of, 185
In Re Quinlin, 20, 231
Inadequacy, sense of, 125
Independence. See Autonomy
Indirect methods, of assisted death, 19–20,
    31
Institutionalization, 227–228, 230
Insurance, possession of lethal medication
    as, 186, 193
Interpersonal dimensions of care, 155
Interrelationships of motivations, 89
Involuntary euthanasia, 22
Isolation, 213

J

Johanson, G., 152
Jonsen, A. R., 220

K

Kass, L. R., 36–37
Kassirer, J. P., 229
Kevorkian, J., 203
Kübler-Ross, E., 221

L

Last act, notion of, 26
Lazy medicine, 27–28
Legal guidance, and qualification for assis-
    tance, 180
Legal status of assisted suicide: and confi-
    dentiality, 162; and existential suffering,
    180; and medication information, 190;
    and value of human life, 219
Lehr, D. E., 203
Levinsky, N. G., 222
Liddle, B., 42
Life-altering conditions, 179
Life-sustaining treatment, withholding of,
    20, 31, 163–164
Loxterkamp, D., 146, 232

M

Malpractice, 200
Managed care, 228–229
Medical technology, age of, 47
Medicare, 222, 226, 227
Medication: asphyxiation in conjunction
    with, 191; dosages of, 190; dual purpose
    of, 203; and emphasis on cure, 159; pos-
    session of, as insurance, 56, 186, 193;
    and providing the means to die,
    189–191; and uncertain lethality, 189
Meier, D. E., 223
Memorial Sloan-Kettering Cancer Center,
    62, 91
Mental health professionals: and communi-
    cation, 155–156; and decision tree,
    151–154; and professional risk, 210; and
    referral of terminally ill or incurable pa-
    tient, 207–212; and role confusion, 5;
    and topic of disclosure, 209
Mercy: idea of, 24; limits of, 21–22; and lazy
    medicine, 27–28
Metastatic cancer, 223
Michigan, 203
Miller, F. G., 26, 34, 35, 224
Model State Act to Authorize and Regulate
    Physician-assisted Suicide, A (Baron),
    185
Morphine, 26, 159, 162–163, 164
Morphine pump, 162–163